Curb Rights

Daniel B. Klein
Adrian Moore
Binyam Reja

CURB RIGHTS

A FOUNDATION FOR FREE
ENTERPRISE IN URBAN TRANSIT

Brookings Institution Press
Washington, D.C.

Copyright © 1997

THE BROOKINGS INSTITUTION

1775 Massachusetts Avenue, N.W., Washington, D.C. 20036

Library of Congress Cataloging-in-Publication Data
Klein, Daniel B.
   Curb rights : a foundation for free enterprise in urban transit /
Daniel B. Klein, Adrian Moore, Binyam Reja.
     p. cm.
   Includes bibliographical references and index.
   ISBN 0-8157-4940-6.—ISBN 0-8157-4939-2 (pbk.)
   1. Local transit—Government policy—United States. 2. Free
enterprise—United Sates. 3. Right of property—United States.
4. Local transit—Government policy—Great Britain. 5. Free
enterprise—Great Britain. 6. Right of property—Great Britain.
I. Moore, Adrian. II. Reja, Binyam. III. Title.
HE4461.K58 1997
388.4′0973—dc21
                                                                    96-45843
                                                                      CIP

9 8 7 6 5 4 3 2 1

Typeset in Palatino

Composition by Linda C. Humphrey
Arlington, Virginia

Printed by R. R. Donnelley and Sons, Co.
Harrisonburg, Virginia

Acknowledgments

This study emerges from years of discussion and study among the authors and especially two University of California–Irvine graduate students, Pia Koskenoja and James Nolan. Their insights and enthusiasm will have been crucial to whatever success the study finds. The authors have also received valuable comments and criticisms from David Anderson, Tyler Cowen, Pete Fielding, Sabrina Gates-Shaffer, Amihai Glazer, Peter Gordon, Charles Lave, John Meyer, Gabriel Roth, two anonymous referees, and especially Linda Cohen, Teri Moore, and Ken Small. For financial support, the authors thank the California Department of Transportation (contract RTA-65V450), and the University of California Transportation Center.

James Schneider edited the book, Gerard Trimarco verified its factual content, Carlotta Ribar proofread it, and Mary Mortensen compiled the index.

Contents

viii   Contents

Contents ix

BREN—Pronounced bren, to rhyme with "wren." German: *brennen,* "to burn." Someone of great energy, vivacity, competence and optimism; a "fireball."

On his first day as a bus driver, Maxey Eckstein handed in receipts of $65. The next day his take was $67. The third day's income was $62. But on the fourth day, Eckstein, a *bren,* emptied no less that $283 on the desk before the cashier.

"Eckstein!" exclaimed the cashier. "This is fantastic. That route never brought in money like this! What happened?"

"Well, after three days on that *cockamamy* route, I figured business would never improve, so I drove over to Fourteenth Street and worked there. I tell you, that street is a gold mine!"

Leo Rosten, The Joys of Yiddish

The functioning of a competition . . . depends, above all, on the existence of an appropriate legal system, a legal system designed both to preserve competition and to make it operate as beneficially as possible.

Friedrich Hayek, The Road to Serdom

Chapter 1

Introduction

In the United States, traditional transit services have long been in decline. The share of all trips that go by transit continues to fall, productivity has declined, and operating deficits have widened. The traditional approaches to running transit systems—government planning or operation of bus and rail, government subsidization of private operations, and heavy regulation of all transit modes, including taxis and shuttle vans—have failed, and the failures have become too great and too ubiquitous to ignore or to permit much hope of their coming right. A growing number of planners and policymakers are readdressing transit policy.

This book is concerned with street-based transit—buses, jitneys, shuttles—not with rail transit. We believe that it is time to rethink the fundamental purpose and structure of transit policy. It is appropriate to place the effort within a broad discussion of the basic forms of governance in society. Arrangements for social governance may be placed along a continuum from government direction at one end to free enterprise at the other. Any given policy arrangement might be reformed to move it in either direction, and movement in either direction will have its advantages and drawbacks. There are trade-offs between the imperfections of government direction and imperfections of the free market.

We maintain that America needs to reform transit in the direction of free enterprise. Yet this reform depends on government action to establish a system of governance that will lead to market success. Transit policymakers need to discover a legal framework within which a system of free enterprise will function. Although the imperfections of government direction are serious, our advocacy of creative government action is *not* undermined by them. We want a form of government action that would be highly decentralized and informed

1

by the comparison of local experiments. Furthermore, short of full privatization of all city streets, transit policy is bound to remain within the province of government regardless of whether policy follows traditional forms, our proposed reforms, or some others. Thus, although the results of our proposed reforms would be subject to the pitfalls of government action, our proposals minimize the scope and severity of those pitfalls.

Figure 1-1 shows the limits of the continuum of social governance. Government direction of affairs is achieved by direct government ownership of resources or by the issuance of regulations that tell private persons what they may or may not do with their property. The other extreme of social governance is free enterprise, in which autonomous individuals choose to interact and exchange as they see fit. The result is a spontaneous order, but an order that depends on a system of property rights. Property rights tell you, not what you may or may not do with your property, but rather what *others* may or may not do with your property. What prevents you from filling in a swamp on your land is a regulation. What prevents others from trespassing to hunt ducks on your land is a property right.

The spontaneous order of free enterprise has been celebrated by Adam Smith, Friedrich Hayek, and other theorists. Following the teachings of Smith and Hayek, economists have explained how in normal market settings—the province of the butcher, the brewer, and the baker—the invisible hand of free enterprise performs better than do alternative governance arrangements. This comparative success is the result notably of two factors that find great vitality in free markets: competition and entrepreneurship. These two factors are often used to advocate deregulation and privatization of services that have slipped too far toward the government end of the continuum.

But a lesson of Smith and Hayek not so well learned is that the success of a spontaneous order depends critically on the property rights framework within which it operates. To call merely for deregulation and privatization requires that the property rights framework for the free-market arrangement is self-evident and functional. Such is not the case in transit services. Many of the primary resources of the industry—roads, bus turnouts, bus stops, sidewalks—are government property and must function within a system of government resources. Because the property rights alternatives for transit services

FIGURE 1-1. *Limiting Cases for the Continuum of Social Governance*

Regulation or government ownership	*Property rights*
Regulation tells you what you may or may not do with your property	Property rights tell others what they may and may not do with your property
Order created by central direction, regulation, or government enterprise	Order emerges from decentralized interaction within property rights framework

are not self-evident, our proposed reforms go beyond simple deregulation and privatization.

Our goal is to reveal how the forms and effectiveness of transit services depend on the character of property rights as they exist in transit markets. We examine a number of transit markets: current markets in the United States, bus markets in Britain where services have been deregulated and privatized, and jitney markets as they have functioned in the United States, past and present, and in the less developed countries. Many of these markets show a tendency toward low levels of competition, and this tendency can be traced to deficiencies of property rights arrangements.

A further goal is to use what we learn about the status of property rights in existing transit markets to devise new forms of governance for transit. Our reform proposals aim at bringing to transit markets the kinds of competition and entrepreneurship that operate in other markets. The nub of our proposals is to establish clear property rights in curb zones, bus turnouts, and bus stops, creating a system of "curb rights." The resources represented by the curb, the loading area, the turnout, and so on could then be managed effectively by private enterprise, and bona fide on-the-road competition could function smoothly. Transit services would be left to emerge in entrepreneurial fashion within the curb rights framework established by local officials.

This book neither advocates nor attacks the idea of public transit. Rather, it explains how market forces can revitalize transit in the face of competition from the automobile. In the next chapter we discusses the triumph of the automobile, a triumph that in the United States will be secure regardless of the course of transit policy. Yet we believe that by making the transit industry more competitive, it would, even after losing its subsidies, probably be bigger and better, especially if the private automobile is made to pay its way. Entrepreneurs would be eager to offer their services, and travelers would find transit more attractive than they do now.

Section One

Diagnosing Traditional Transit

Any proposal for serious reform ought first of all to be grounded in a knowledge and interpretation of the status quo. This section describes two central features of the status quo: the triumph of the automobile and the decline of traditional transit. Then it uses ideas from the discipline of political economy to explain the reasons for the difficulties of traditional transit.

Chapter 2

The Triumph of the Private Automobile

In his 1991 book *Edge City*, Joel Garreau described how Americans have been spreading out in new, low-density edge cities—areas that lack definite urban form yet nonetheless function as cities, providing homes, shopping, and jobs. Edge cities are one consequence of prosperity and the rise of the private automobile. As people get wealthier and can afford a car for every driver, they can reside farther from city activities, and they want more space to spread out. "Edgification" is most advanced in the United States, but it is the natural process for any country that grows wealthy.

The triumph of the automobile is also affecting how researchers think about urban transit. Within the realm of policy and funding, different types of transit continue to vie with one another, but all must face the reality that the transit pie is shrinking. In America 90 percent of the people of driving age in 1991 were licensed drivers, and 89 percent of licensed drivers had access to an automobile.[1] In 1990 about 94 percent of all trips went by auto, van, or pickup.[2] The reasons for the triumph are simple: the auto is far superior in flexibility, privacy, accommodation of diverse lifestyles, speed, and access to all points known to man and pavement. Even such critics of America's automobile culture as James Flink recognize the auto's triumph.[3] Observers do disagree over whether government subsidization of auto use has exceeded subsidization of transit use.[4] We suggest that both kinds of transportation be made, as far as practical, to pay their own way. At any rate, Americans must live with the results of what is past, and we believe that the automobile would have prevailed even without subsidies.

1. Webber (1994).
2. Nationwide Personal Transportation Survey (1990).
3. Flink (1988).
4. Flink (1988); Pucher (1993a, b); Beshers (1994).

Of course, the triumph of the auto has brought its own problems. Certainly, much has been made of the problem of congestion. But Charles Lave has pointed out that demographic trends give reason to believe that, as his title has it, "Things Won't Get A Lot Worse." And in fact commuting travel times seem to have declined between 1980 and 1985 in all but two of the twenty largest U.S. metropolitan areas.[5] Congestion on surface streets is being reduced somewhat by the use of traffic sensors and smart technologies. On highways, congestion can now be managed by using electronic toll collection and charging higher tolls at peak periods.[6] Charging tolls on all highways would also help end the policy of subsidizing auto use.

The other chief problem with the automobile is air pollution. Many transportation planners have sought to reduce auto emissions and rush hour traffic by creating incentives to carpool, ride transit, work at home, and shift work schedules away from peak hours. Such programs—known as "transportation demand management"—have achieved little.[7] Driven by the 1990 Clean Air Act, employers have been required to provide incentives to their employees to reduce solo driving to work. These programs have proven very costly and have had almost no effect on commuter travel decisions.[8] Even efforts aimed directly at making it inconvenient to drive have had little effect.

Many other regulatory policies have taken aim at auto emissions. Emission standards are imposed on automakers, motorists are required to bring their cars for emissions inspections, and cleaner burning fuels are mandated. Again technology has steadily reduced the problem and has recently promised a powerful solution, a solution in line with the property rights approach: remote sensing of tailpipe emissions can police the act of emitting by an individual vehicle and keep those with high emissions off the road.[9]

Over time, people find automobiles ever more affordable, and the problems created by automobiles are becoming ever more manageable. Transit thus takes its place at the edge of the automobile's domain—an ever narrowing edge. The real transit issue has not been

5. Gordon, Richardson, and Jun (1991), p. 418.
6. Gómez-Ibáñez and Small (1994).
7. Brownstone and Golob (1992); Giuliano (1992); Kuzmyak and Schreffler (1993).
8. Giuliano, Hwang, and Wachs (1993); Green (1995).
9. Lawson (1993, 1995); Klein and Koskenoja (1996).

bus versus rail, but transit versus the automobile. It is time that transit surrender the contest and seek a humble accord.

If the automobile is transit's vanquisher, it may also be its mentor, for it may show transit how to salvage its future. Research on mode choice shows that travelers value the following characteristics: short trip times, avoidance of transfers and waiting time, door-to-door service, reliability, comfort, seat availability, storage space, security, and flexibility.[10] Also of importance are psychological factors such as privacy and autonomy.[11] The auto consistently surpasses existing transit modes in providing all these appealing travel characteristics. The only desirable characteristics not readily associated with the automobile are accident safety, exposure to social interaction, and the ability to read or sleep or whatnot while traveling. Overall, various studies show that the car offers the superior bundle of mode characteristics.[12] As Melvin Webber has argued in "The Joys of Automobility," if transit is to compete it must emulate the private automobile.[13] Our property rights proposal would favor transit services more like the private automobile, blurring the distinction between the private car and mass transportation.

10. For short trip times, see Brown (1972); Golob and others (1972); Dobson and Nicolaidis (1974); Hensher, McLeod, and Stanley (1975); Johnson (1978); Weismann (1981); Wachs (1992). For door-to-door service, see Flannelly and others (1991); reliability, Olsen and Smith (1973); comfort, Chou (1992); seat availability, Flannelly and others (1991); storage space and security, Levine and Wachs (1986); flexibility, Flannelly and others (1991).

11. Tehan and Wachs (1972); Olsen and Smith (1973).

12. Hensher, McLeod, and Stanley (1975); Johnson (1978); Orski (1990).

13. Webber (1992).

Chapter 3

The Fizzle of Traditional Transit

The story of public transit's decline begins in the early part of the twentieth century, when it was in robust health. Electric streetcars became the dominant form of transit, supplanting the slower and less efficient horsecars long familiar in large and medium-sized cities. To allow the streetcar companies to recoup capital costs, local governments granted them route monopolies and regulated them as natural monopolies. The structure of monopoly regulation was inflexible to changes in demand and technology.

These arrangements worked well for decades. The Second World War, however, witnessed a vast expansion of the labor force and a corresponding increase in transit ridership. But government regulations did not allow transit companies to raise fares; they had to meet the increased demand by running vehicles overtime. As equipment deteriorated the constraints posed by wartime rationing prevented the companies from replacing vehicles and track. After the war the streetcar companies spent a great deal of capital on replacement as ridership declined, but regulators continued to hinder them from reducing service or raising fares.[1]

By the 1950s public transit had shifted from depending on streetcars to depending mainly on motorbuses. Motorbus technology does not lend itself to increasing returns and natural monopoly, but the regulatory structure of the streetcars stayed the same. As George Hilton commented in "The Rise and Decline of Monopolized Transit," the regulatory constraints on raising fares concomitant with monopoly

1. Adler (1991).

franchise should bear much of the blame for the eventual demise of the private operators.[2]

As household income increased, people bought cars and moved to the suburbs. Fewer people rode public transit, but transit had to cover more ground. As a result, it became less able to pay for itself and, in the 1950s and 1960s, most transit companies went bankrupt. To save city transit systems, Congress passed the Urban Mass Transportation Act in 1964, providing funds for local governments to purchase transit systems. Municipalities responded by purchasing the private companies and setting up their own local or regional agencies to operate mass transit.

The market trend since the 1960s has been against public transit. Transit's share of commuter trips declined from 12.6 percent in 1969 to 5.1 percent in 1990 (table 3-1). Passenger bus trips have decreased in absolute terms, but the decrease is not apparent in table 3-1 because in 1980 statisticians began counting a journey with a transfer as two trips rather than one, and there was an extreme peak in real gas prices that caused many travelers temporarily to switch to transit.[3] Meanwhile, passenger rail trips increased between 1980 and 1990 because of the construction of new rail systems, particularly in Washington, D. C., and the Bay Area. Between 1990 and 1992, however, the underlying trend asserted itself and rail ridership fell (table 3-1).

There is no shame in market contraction. It is part of a dynamic mix of competition, rising incomes, and technological change. The trouble, however, is that the transit industry has not adjusted appropriately. Since the 1960s suburbanization has stretched development beyond the areas traditionally served by transit.[4] Suburban residents have pressured transit agencies to expand service to their communities.[5] As a result, vehicle miles for all modes increased by 60 percent between 1970 and 1992; new services in the suburbs account for most of this increase. Yet passenger miles remained roughly constant because the suburban communities make least use of public transit. Now there are a lot more near-empty buses on the road. In 1980 there were, on average, 13 passengers per bus (with a capacity of 70, seated

2. Hilton (1985, 34–37).

3. Beesley and Kemp (1987, p. 1038); Department of Transportation (1995, p. 189).

4. Cervero (1986, p. 103).

5. Sale and Green (1979, p. 23); Congressional Budget Office (1988, p. 41).

TABLE 3-1. *Transit Ridership and Passenger Miles, Selected Years, 1960–92*

Millions unless otherwise specified

Passenger trips and vehicle miles	1960	1970	1980	1990	1992
Passenger trips[a]	8,734	7,150	8,358	8,526	8,226
Rail[b]	2,313	2,116	2,521	2,849	2,709
Bus	6,425	5,034	5,837	5,677	5,517
Vehicle miles	2,042.1	1,850.1	2,258.4	2,903.5	2,950.8
Rail[b]	465.7	440.8	581.2	773.6	772.8
Bus	1,576.4	1,409.3	1,677.2	2,129.9	2178
Passenger miles	n.a.	n.a.	39,245	40,109	39,094
Rail[b]	n.a.	n.a.	17,455	19,128	18,758
Bus	n.a.	n.a.	21,790	20,981	20,336
Passengers per vehicle					
Rail[b]	n.a.	n.a.	30.0	24.7	24.3
Bus	n.a.	n.a.	13.0	9.9	9.3
	1969[c]	1977	1983	1990	1992
Transit share of commuter trips (percent)	12.6	8.5	6.2	5.1	n.a.
Transit share of total person trips (percent)	3.4	2.7	2.7	2.2	n.a.

Sources: American Public Transit Association (1993); Federal Transit Authority (1994); Nationwide Personal Transportation Survey (1990).

n.a. Not available.

a. Starting in 1980, passenger trips were unlinked, as reported in American Public Transit Association (1993) and Federal Transit Authority (1994).

b. Includes light rail, heavy rail, and commuter rail.

c. NPTS data.

and standing). By 1992 the figure was down to 9.3 passengers (and average bus capacity had not changed much).[6] These figures are aggregate measures that include rush hour traffic. Off-peak buses often run virtually empty. Simply put, public transit authorities have tended to overprovide their service.

Financial trends for transit services are even more discouraging.

6. American Public Transit Association (1993).

Although passenger trips for all modes have declined substantially since 1960, operating costs have increased in real terms by 160 percent (table 3-2 and figure 3-1). A comparison of passenger trips and operating costs is provided in figure 3.2. The largest share of operating costs goes to labor compensation, which has increased from 66 percent to 75 percent (table 3-2). Operating costs per passenger trip increased 175 percent between 1960 and 1992. And the annualized capital cost has been even bleaker: in twelve years (1980 to 1992) the real cost of producing a passenger trip increased by 45 percent. Relative to productivity trends in other service industries, this performance must be deemed poor.[7]

Earnings from passenger fares and other operating revenues have declined consistently except in the 1980s when new rail systems were completed. The ratio of earnings to operating costs decreased from 1.03 in 1960 to 0.37 in 1992 (table 3-2). The rate of deficit expansion is even worse when capital costs are included: between 1980 and 1992 the ratio of earnings to total annualized costs fell from 0.39 to 0.31. Just two generations ago transit was earning its income from paying customers in the private enterprise economy. Today, about 70 percent of its money comes from taxpayers. And tax dollars, remember, are expensive dollars in that there are high transaction costs and distortions associated with the tax system; the Office of Management and Budget advises that government expenditures be multiplied by 1.25 to reflect these excess burdens.[8]

Some would maintain that declining productivity does not damn public transit. There are also some ancillary justifications that often favor it: the reduction of congestion, air pollution, and energy use. But again, the record shows a fizzling of hopes. Except in dense metropolitan areas, the subsidization of transit has no significant impact on congestion. Transit's share of commuter trips has been steadily shrinking (table 3-1). More telling, by 1990 transit's share of total trips had decreased to 2 percent.[9] In addition, in *Stuck in Traffic* Anthony Downs reminds us that for an unpriced facility such as a freeway (as opposed to a toll road), any short-run abatement of congestion brings out some latent demand to use the less congested facility.[10] As for air pollution,

7. Baumol (1967).
8. Office of Management and Budget (1992, p. 10).
9. Nationwide Personal Transportation Survey (1990, pp. 4-4, 4-39).
10. Downs (1992, p. 27).

TABLE 3-2. *Transit Costs and Revenues, Selected Years, 1960–92*
1992 dollars unless otherwise specified

Costs and revenues	1960	1970	1980	1990	1992
Costs					
Operating costs (millions)	6,114.6	6,841.5	12,663.5	15,991.5	15,913.2
Rail	n.a.	n.a.	4,330.7	6,438.6	6,032.0
Bus	n.a.	n.a.	8,332.8	9,552.9	9,881.2
Annualized capital cost, all modes[a] (millions)	n.a.	n.a.	790.2	2,448.6	3,252.2
Total annualized cost (operating and capital) (millions)	n.a.	n.a.	13,453.7	18,440.1	19,165.4
Total labor cost (salaries and benefits) (millions)	4,062.2	4,606.8	7,891.7	12,030.8	11,989.1
Labor share of operating cost (percent)	66	67	62	75	75
Operating cost per passenger trip	0.70	0.96	1.52	1.88	1.93
Rail	n.a.	n.a.	1.72	2.26	2.23
Bus	n.a.	n.a.	1.43	1.68	1.79
Operating cost per vehicle mile	2.99	3.70	5.61	5.51	5.39
Rail	n.a.	n.a.	7.45	8.32	7.81
Bus	n.a.	n.a	4.97	4.49	4.54
Total annualized cost per passenger trip, all modes	n.a.	n.a.	1.61	2.16	2.33
Total annualized cost per vehicle mile, all modes	n.a.	n.a.	5.96	6.35	6.49
Revenue (millions)					
Earnings	6,282.0	6,060.1	5,282.7	6,161.6	5,957.0
Rail	1,751.0	1,589.6	2,048.7	2,978.2	2,898.2
Bus	4,531.0	4,470.5	3,234.0	3,183.4	3,058.8
Earnings ÷ operating cost	1.03	0.89	0.42	0.39	0.37
Rail	n.a.	n.a.	0.47	0.46	0.48
Bus	n.a.	n.a.	0.39	0.33	0.31
Earnings ÷ total annualized cost, all modes	n.a.	n.a.	0.39	0.33	0.31

Sources: See table 3-1.
n.a. Not available.
a. Depreciation, amortization, interest payments, and other reconciling items for that year.

FIGURE 3-1. *Total Public Transit Operating Costs and Passenger Trips, Selected Years, 1960–92*

Millions of trips or dollars

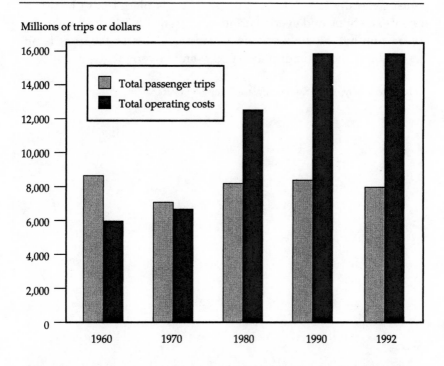

Sources: Tables 3-1 and 3-2. In 1980 statisticians began counting trips with a transfer as two trips, thus the upsurge in total trips starting that year.

emission comparisons between autos and transit vehicles have shown that transit vehicles emit less per passenger mile.[11] But again, because public transit's share of total passenger miles is so small, the contribution is insignificant. On the matter of energy conservation, transit is again no help. Robert Cervero and Gordon Fielding have shown that, based on actual ridership, transit consumes far more energy than autos per passenger trip.[12] According to the 1993 *Transportation Energy Data Book* the average automobile consumes 3,593 BTUs per passenger mile, while the average transit bus consumes 4,374 and the average rail system 3,687. When the energy use of construction is factored in, rail systems are extravagant energy users.[13]

11. Lowe (1990, p. 14).
12. Cervero (1983, p. 16); Fielding (1995).
13. Lave (1977); Altshuler (1979, p. 159); Lowe (1990, p. 13).

The transit market is contracting because of natural forces. What is unfortunate is that public policy has not allowed the industry to adjust naturally to the trends; instead, it has placed false hopes in transit. The hype and even mythology of transit has turned a natural contraction into an embarrassment and scandal.[14] The reasons lie in the troubled operation of public policy and government enterprise.

14. For the hype and mythology, see Richmond (forthcoming).

Chapter 4

Why Traditional Transit Fizzles

There are two bodies of thought that can help explain why traditional urban transit arrangements fizzle. The first is the Austrian economic perspective associated with Friedrich Hayek that emphasizes the importance of understanding local conditions. This approach tends to assume for the sake of analysis that public officials are exceptionally scrupulous and diligent. The second is the "public choice" learning that explores the ways in which incentives interact with ordinary self-regarding interest to influence government behavior. This school of thought insists that public officials are not especially scrupulous, but rather are like everybody else. We will begin our diagnosis of traditional urban transit with an application of the Hayekian insights.

A Hayekian Critique of Traditional Urban Transit

Let us suppose that a central authority faces the task of planning the entire bus system for a large metropolitan area. Centralization makes it easier to integrate service, coordinate the parts, and ensure reliable schedules. But the economic terrain consists of conditions that are highly particularistic and constantly changing. It is in this conection that Hayek warned, "as the area of unified planning is extended, particular knowledge of local circumstances will, of necessity, be less effectively used."[1]

Consider the desires of transit consumers. They care about where they have to go to catch the bus, how long they will have to wait for

---

1. Hayek (1960, p. 352).

it, and where it will take them. They care about characteristics of the journey: the speed, whether there is much stopping, and whether they will have to make transfers. Then there are the characteristics associated with the bus: air conditioning, seat availability, privacy in seating, legroom, comfort for reading or sleeping, storage space, and peace and quiet. Consumers care about the image of being a transit user and whether the driver is friendly and helpful. And they always want to feel safe. Consumer preference for these facets of service will, furthermore, vary by neighborhood, time of day, weather, season, occurrence of special events, and many other factors.

For service providers there are again a number of factors to consider: the routes to follow, schedules, whether to permit courtesy deviations, types of vehicles to use, special features on board, personnel training, management of the system, maintenance of vehicles, and so on. There is also the matter of pricing the service. Paul Kerin warns of the formidability of establishing socially optimal fares:

> extremely complex interrelationships must be taken into account in order to determine an efficient set of transit fares. For example, one needs to be aware of the implications of fares strategy for transit ridership, costs, and subsidy requirements, usage of alternative modes, the level and location of traffic congestion, noise and air pollution, energy usage, the need for additional road capacity, the long-run dynamic effects on the location decisions of firms and households, managerial and worker incentive effects, and so on.[2]

The planners' responsibility is not to determine performance standards for each of these facets as a separate matter, but to settle on broad institutional arrangements that will establish the skeleton of how things will be done. Planners consider alternative institutional arrangements, and each possible arrangement carries a different set of implications for all the particulars of operation and for the future evolution of the agency. The implications are only very dimly perceived when fundamental choices are made. In finally settling on a plan, the planners must weigh one alternative against another according to how well they are likely to do in achieving some mixture of social and administrative goals. Two notable features mark the

2. Kerin (1992, p. 42).

planners' problem: first, at some point they must decide when to stop searching for additional arrangements to consider; and second, they must finally decide on one arrangement without much knowledge of how it will work out in all the particulars.

Once a broad plan is outlined and implemented, the agency begins to accumulate experience. Its operations are like tendrils touching the local conditions they meet. But compared with the free market, the tendrils of the public agency have three limitations: a lack of reach, a lack of sensation, and a lack of responsiveness.

First, because a centralized public system will not brook transit competition—either regulation will keep competitors out or subsidization of the public system will deter them—it is exclusively the tendrils of the public monopoly that reach into the local particulars. This is in fundamental contrast to an open market, in which there are many potential entrants. Tendrils in taxi services, van services, private bus companies, vanpool services, package delivery, hotels, parking lots, shopping centers, or myriad other sources could deliver superior understanding of local conditions and could turn up profit opportunities. In an open market, individuals and groups from all these sources have the potential to bring their knowledge of local conditions to bear on the evolution of local transit services. But when transit is monopolized by law, these tendrils are eradicated, and the reach of knowledge into local conditions is much more limited.

Second, in the contact it does have with local conditions, the public agency lacks sensation: it learns little about the local markets it touches. Even though bus drivers come into contact with local conditions, they do not explore the possibilities of what they learn. Furthermore, whatever knowledge they and other employees attain is not conveyed very well to the executives of a large integrated transit system. Because the executives must manage the system as a whole, they will follow procedures—staff discussions, public hearings, surveys, and other formalized modes of information gathering—that lack sensitivity to local conditions and special insights. In a competitive and decentralized system, entrepreneurs dig deeper into local conditions. Their experiments—including their failures—make use of local knowledge to an extent that no amount of fact finding can.

Third, the public agency is inevitably less responsive than free enterprise. Even if officials are knowledgeable about local conditions, they are still very limited in their ability to revise the system. Centralized organizations dislike change and conflict, and the business-as-usual outlook is tenacious. With a strong organizational orientation toward integration of transit services, the bureaucracy is not inclined to attempt piecemeal experimentation or flexible responses to new conditions. Even if officials were readily able to respond to new information, they would probably lack the incentive to do so. In a free, competitive market, good service brings an increase in funding (from consumers); bad service repels consumers and the provider either perishes or shapes up.[3] But in a government agency, service quality is generally neither rewarded nor punished by the legislators and others who make funding decisions. Bad service may even be met by increases in funding. Agency officials therefore may often not respond to whatever knowledge of local conditions they do have.

A lack of responsive action feeds back into a lack of knowledge. Israel Kirzner has explained that discovery of opportunity often takes place only because a person has an incentive to remain alert to new insights.[4] If public officials lack incentive, either because they cannot personally gain from action or because they would be frustrated in their efforts to implement change, they are unlikely to search out information or to achieve new insights. Where action is lumbering and sluggish, alertness gets switched off. Stiff joints and weak muscles are both conditions that call for exercise, but each may inhibit improvement in the other.

In Hayek's view of the free market, it is the market itself that generates new perceptions by participants. By taking action, the individual affects market conditions—notably, but not exclusively, current prices—that in turn influence other individuals' perceptions of opportunity and lead to their taking action. The interplay of knowledge and the free market can be characterized in three observations:

— the free market is effective in making use of the existing, dispersed knowledge of local conditions;

— by giving individuals the freedom to enter, exit, and contract, the free market permits them flexibility in responding to perceived *changes* in the conditions;

— by pressing entrepreneurs into contact and experimentation with local conditions and by giving them an interest in achieving new insights, the free market fuels the discovery of opportunities that had gone unnoticed.

3. Alchian (1950).
4. Kirzner (1985).

These functions are all part of what Hayek called the discovery process. In contrast, a market served by a protected monopolistic organization is largely innocent of this dialectic of discovery.

The importance of Hayek's point is hard to assess—inherently so. To measure how well local opportunity is exploited, the investigator would have to know about the local opportunity that goes unexploited, which is precisely what eludes knowing. Certain comparisons, however, may illustrate Hayek's line of argument. Local knowledge is important not only in finding new services and markets, but in finding ways to reduce costs. Discovery and innovation, which are never the hallmarks of government agencies, are so important in enhancing efficiency that some observers have concluded that private and deregulated industries, even with relatively little competition, are more efficient than public enterprises or regulated markets, even under the best real-world conditions.[5]

The advantages that private companies have in using knowledge of local conditions are reflected in cost comparisons of public and private ownership of transit. Studies show greater efficiency in the private firms and less rapid escalation in costs during the past thirty years.[6] One study estimates that private transit systems have succeeded in providing 20 to 50 percent more service per dollar of cost than have public systems.[7] These systems are in many cases regulated or subsidized private monopolies, so the comparisons cannot be considered a test between central planning and the free market. Nonetheless, the greater efficiency suggests the importance of incentive to discover and adopt ways of reducing costs.

Hayekian teachings about free enterprise rest on a crucial presupposition: that a sensible system of property rights underlies the market. Where property rights are lacking or ill defined, the spontaneous order stemming from local opportunity will not function. There may be an undertaking that, if carried out, would benefit society as a whole, but because property rights are ill defined no entrepreneur will perceive a personal advantage in pursuing it.

In contrast to traditional transit policies, a property rights approach favors policies that promote efficiency and discovery by fa-

5. Armstrong, Cowan, and Vickers (1994, p. 111ff); Primeaux (1976).

6. Pashigian (1976); Pucher, Markstedt, and Hirschman (1983); Morlok and Viton (1985).

7. Tramontozzi and Chilton (1987, p. 26).

voring property rights not only in transit vehicles but also in *curbspace* (and adjoining sidewalk area). We shall later develop the idea of curb rights. Free enterprise makes a good banner; as Will Rogers said, "Freedom doesn't work as well in practice as it does in speeches." To work in practice, freedom must be understood within a system of property rights, and in some cases the creation of such a system calls for creativity and judgment. Once a good system of property rights is established for transit, the survival and expansion of services would depend on the judgment of paying customers, not public officials.

A Public Choice Critique of Traditional Urban Transit

There used to be a tendency among academic economists to identify imperfections of the free market and declare them market failures, as though the mere existence of such imperfections provided grounds for government intervention. This tendency was strong after World War II, when abstract model building became the valid manner of economic discourse. This style of discourse lent itself to the study of buying and selling, but not of persuasion and politics. Thus government was spared blackboard dissection and academic scrutiny and kept its popular image as the people's servant. But the situation started to change in the 1960s when James Buchanan, Gordon Tullock, Ronald Coase, and other economists applied their logic of choice and incentives to behavior in the public sector.[8] Their careful scrutiny uncovered many imperfections in government as well. Thanks to public choice research, which has flourished academically and won Nobel laurels, economists are now much more attentive to the idea that corrective government action may well show imperfections more severe than those of free enterprise.

Private enterprise works toward profit, but the same cannot be said about government agencies. What then are the goals of public agencies? No single goal stands out, generally speaking, except that of serving the public. This is the official goal, but its ambiguity becomes evident when one tries to translate it into specifics. The specific actions that best serve the public, and how to go about them, must still be decided. Moreover, lurking behind the official goal are

8.   Buchanan and Tullock (1962).

the personal goals of the public servants, and the two are not always well aligned.

When one looks at specifics, the official goals of a transit agency are multiple, confused, and conflicted. The obvious goal is to provide mobility, especially to those who do not have alternative means of travel. But other official goals tread on this basic goal. In fact, the original justification for federal funding of public transit was not mobility but urban renewal. By 1960 cities and states could no longer afford to build or expand transit systems. The Public Works Committee of Congress did not think that improved mobility called for transit; that goal would be met by highways. So city officials persuaded a different congressional committee that transit would stimulate urban renewal.[9] And in 1961 the Housing Act gave cities $75 million to begin buying failing transit companies.[10]

Since then, one of the powerful official goals of public transit has been to maintain the downtowns. In fact, in 1978 the Urban Mass Transportation Administration specified that new rail systems must give preference to serving densely populated downtown areas. This goal competes with the goal of assisting mobility in two ways. First, it often gives life to rail projects and diverts transit money away from bus service, which dollar for dollar provides much more mobility. Second, the downtown orientation favors a radial route structure (for bus or rail), whereas in today's polycentric urban areas a network structure would better connect the parts.

The emphasis on serving the downtown, however, is merely one of a proliferation of goals. Another has become satisfying suburban taxpayers who lobby for services in their areas. Transit agencies have generally responded by extending the radial system into lightly traveled suburban areas, even though again a network system would better meet their needs.

During the past twenty-five years, these goals have been joined by energy conservation, cleaner air, reduced congestion, and alleviation of poverty. Whereas the goals of private sector agents are few and frank, the goals of public officials are many and murky.

To understand a bureaucrat's behavior, one needs to know his official goals, personal goals, and the institutional structure in which he

9. Jones (1985).
10. Meyer and Gómez-Ibáñez (1981, pp. 41–43).

FIGURE 4-1. *The Circle of Goals, Incentives, and Action for Public Officials*

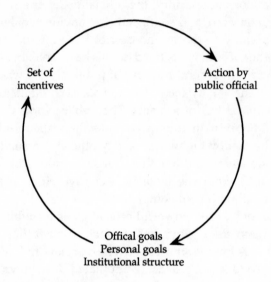

Set of
incentives

Action by
public official

Offical goals
Personal goals
Institutional structure

works. These three factors combine to create a set of incentives that induce the bureaucrat to appropriate action, and his action has various consequences, some unintended, which then influence anew the goals and institutional structure (figure 4-1).

Public choice economists are sometimes called cynics because they place the personal goals of civil servants under the microscope. But they are not cynics. They are simply assuming that the person in the public agency is the same as the person buying milk in the supermarket, no better and no worse. Public officials, like everyone else, value personal comfort, security, prestige, and a feeling of being important. They want more money. They may want more time away from work. In their work they may want more pleasure or stimulation or gratification or peace and quiet. Meeting such personal goals will sometimes satisfy official goals, but often it will not. There will be a good deal of hokum and posturing as officials purport to serve one official goal while really pursuing personal goals or some other official goal. Also, there is a tendency for human beings to believe their own press, making official and personal goals conceptually inseparable.[11]

11. Klein (1994).

In 1970 William Niskanen contended that the personal goals of security, advancement, and power create incentives to increase a public agency's budget.[12] He argued that an agency will tend to overproduce its service and inflate its costs. A survey of the best attempts to test these results empirically found support for Niskanen's theory: forty out of the fifty studies examined found public agencies significantly less efficient than private firms providing the same service.[13] When applied to public transit agencies, the theory offers an explanation for the constant effort to increase capacity and service area, to exclude competition, and inflate costs. The theory also helps explain the pattern of grossly exaggerated ridership forecasts, as shown by Melvin Webber's study on the BART system, John Kain's "Deception in Dallas," and Donald Pickerell's "A Desire Named Streetcar."[14] That actual ridership turns out to fill such a small percentage of capacity, even with heavily subsidized fares, also accords with Niskanen's theory of the tendency to overprovide service.[15]

Official goals are further muddled by the demands of special interests. Cities and municipal transit agencies seek state and federal funding; in turn local interests lobby municipal agencies. Meetings of the Los Angeles Metropolitan Transportation Agency, for example, attract more lobbyists than do all the offices of the state legislature in Sacramento.[16] *Rent seeking* is the term applied to lobbying and other activities that seek wealth (or rents) by reshuffling political prerogatives rather than by producing new wealth.[17]

One of the rents in question is the political returns to officials from providing contracts and jobs for new construction projects or local employment in the transit industry.[18] Often one hears about jump-starting the local economy with new construction projects. Rent seeking of this type is a negative-sum game: the resources devoted to lobbying for federal transit money are a net social loss, even when the sought-for redistribution is successful. Because construction rents are substantial for rail and negligible for buses, this form of rent seeking creates a bias toward rail.

12. Niskanen (1971).
13. Mueller (1989, p. 261).
14. Webber (1976); Kain (1990); Pickerell (1992).
15. Kain (1988); Gordon (1989).
16. Kain (1988); Gordon (1989).
17. Tullock (1967).
18. Weingast, Shepsle, and Johnsen (1981).

One of the largest rents (or privileges) associated with public transit comes from section 13(c) of the Urban Mass Transportation Act of 1964. This section prevents a transit agency from taking any action that will have adverse effects on its public transit union employees. Thus the agency may not be free to bring in part-time workers for peak periods, or to contract out services, or to cut back service in weak markets. Section 13(c) gives great power to the transit worker unions and seriously impedes efforts to improve efficiency.[19] Transit agencies must explicitly serve the interests of transit unions when planning services and route structures. Labor's expanding share of transit costs (see table 3-2) is a striking example of how objectives that are extraneous and brazenly self-serving can affect institutional structure and even become official goals of the transit agency.

The transit agency attracts lobbyists, but also acts as lobbyist in seeking subsidies from the state capital or the federal government. Table 4-1 shows sources of transit subsidies by level of government. Because data were kept differently before 1980, the table covers selected years only from 1980 onward, so it does not reflect the fact that subsidy levels were growing in the 1970s as well. Operating subsidies have grown to 60 percent of operating costs, a dominant part of transit budgets. Transit officials thus have increasing incentives to devote resources to lobbying for subsidies. State and federal subsidies often carry various restrictions, and observing these rules takes precedence over local transit needs in determining how the resources are used.

The murkiness of goals and incentives in public agencies often prompts the imposition of rigid rules and procedures on an agency or within it. Those who impose such rules have one objective in mind, but the lack of flexibility thus imposed is later found to impede other worthy goals. For example, California's Transportation Development Act taxes gasoline to pay for public transit and, in the interest of fairness, disburses the funds to the counties such that each gets back what it paid in.[20] The result is that the counties using the most gasoline per capita, and consequently the least transit, get the most transit money. Thus services in these counties are overprovided and resources are wasted on unused transit.

19. Chomitz and Lave (1984); Rottenberg (1985); Love and Cox (1991, p. 14).
20. Eckert (1979); Taylor (1992).

TABLE 4-1. *Public Transit Operating and Capital Subsidies, 1980, 1990, 1992*
Millions of 1992 dollars

	1980	1990	1992
Operating subsidy			
Local	2,901.7	5,728.1	4,747.8
State	1,397.1	3,238.9	3,775.6
Federal	1,863.1	925.8	964.3
Total	6,162.0	9,892.7	9,487.7
Operating subsidy ÷ operating cost	0.49	0.62	0.60
Capital subsidy			
Local	382.3	1,262.8	830.0
State	335.8	747.7	801.0
Federal	2,606.6	3,082.2	2,673.0
Total	3,324.8	5,092.7	4,304.0
Total subsidy (operating + capital)	9,486.7	14,985.4	13,791.7

Sources: American Public Transit Association (1993); Federal Transit Authority (1994); Nationwide Personal Transportation Survey (1990).

Other perversities of public transit funding and administration are more striking. If an organization learns to make its resources go further, it may be that the efficiency gains are not enjoyed as returns to the organization but rather provide a justification for reducing subsidies or fares. In regulated monopolies, regulators tend to transfer efficiency gains to consumers.[21] In technological research, subsidies may be taken away from the more successful firms.[22] In transit funding, discretionary funding tends to go to the agencies that are having the most severe problems with ridership or experiencing the most financial difficulty.[23] And capital subsidies may also encourage transit agencies to retire vehicles prematurely.[24] These policies undercut incentives to reduce costs, make the service more attractive, or earn additional revenue. In the free market the honest dollar selects

21. Armstrong, Cowan, and Vickers (1994, p. 116).
22. Cohen and Noll (1994, p. 63).
23. Jones (1985, p. 155).
24. Meyer and Gómez-Ibáñez (1981, p. 45).

for what works and leaves failed services to reform or die.[25] In the public sector there is no comparable survival mechanism; failing services simply clamor for more funding.

A final perversity of traditional public transit arrangements is their regressivity. Service regressivity appears in the bias toward rail service; the average rail passenger is a suburban commuter and has a higher income than the average bus passenger.[26] Regressivity is also found in the tax burden for public subsidies to transit systems; the tax burden for transit seems to take a larger portion of income from the poor than it does from the rich.[27]

Thus public ownership and the existence of subsidies mean that within transit agencies the direct connection between performance and financial reward is severed, and incentives become diffuse, confused, and disingenuous. Unintended consequences induce new schemes to reform the agency, schemes that do not address the fundamental problem.

Transit officials know that real leadership and a clear sense of priorities will never emerge. Their attitude toward reform proposals is recalcitrance. As Alan Altshuler contended in *The Urban Transportation System*, public transit agencies become strongly biased toward maintaining the status quo. When reform or change is in the air, transit officials attempt to "confine new issues within the narrowest possible bounds and thereby to minimize conflict." They try to avoid having to take anything away from anyone, defining the policy game as one of "winners without losers."[28] The result is consensus politics and the staving off of significant change.[29] When change does occur, it is usually in response to a real or supposed crisis. This may indeed alter the status quo, but not the status quo bias.

The bias toward the status quo leads to increased agency intervention in transit operations. Once officials have monopolized the industry, citizens must turn to them for remedies to their transit troubles; they cannot turn to competitors. Officials respond with further regulations in an effort to patch up the perceived problem. Thus intervention begets intervention, in a dynamic fueled by officials' desire not

25. Alchian (1950).
26. Gross (1995).
27. Straszheim (1979); Hodge (1988); Hay (1993).
28. Altshuler (1979, p. 12).
29. Cervero (1996, p. 164).

to rock the boat.[30] The taxi industry is subject to this intervention dynamic, and a similar cycle occurs in bus service in many less developed countries.[31] Illegal private bus drivers form associations and seek official recognition to guard against interloping on their routes. But official recognition means regulation, deteriorating service quality, and finally a new generation of interlopers. And the pattern repeats itself. The dynamic produces, at most times, creeping regulatory changes to the status quo, until finally the industry reaches a crisis, and drastic changes in policy are made.

In *Going Private* José Gómez-Ibáñez and John Meyer portrayed a cycle of private and public involvement in transit. They contended that the intervention dynamic leads to the decline of the industry, public takeover, further decline, and finally reprivatization, bringing the situation back to the starting point.[32] Bus service in Kingston, Jamaica, provides an example. By 1974, after twenty years of operations, government regulations and service mandates had bankrupted the private company. The city took over the system, but costs became exorbitant, and in 1983 they privatized and deregulated the market.[33] We propose a way to break from the cycle, by having transit governed by a system of property rights, not by regulation.

30. Mises (1978).
31. For the taxi industry see Frankena and Pautler (1986a, b). For buses see De Soto (1989); Diandas and Roth (1995).
32. Gómez-Ibáñez and Meyer (1993, p. 17).
33. World Bank (1988).

Section Two

Transit Markets Improperly Regulated and Improperly Deregulated

Transit services are delivered in public places on public property. Therefore, even when provided by private enterprise the services must work in conjunction with rules governing government resources. But the rules appropriate for transit operations are by no means self-evident and invariant to particulars of the locale. Experiments in regulation, deregulation, and privatization often turn out differently from what was expected because the rules turn out to be deficient in some manner. In this section we review a diversity of transit experiences. These experiences often show a deficiency of secure property rights, creating a sort of tragedy of the commons, and the result is movement toward unified management of the commons. The result is often unified control over the commons: cartels or monopolies come to possess uncontested control over transit routes.

We review ten transit experiences to understand the deficiencies of the property rights arrangements and to learn how better arrangements might be devised. The experiences can be organized into three categories of transit service in an urban transit typology based on whether service follows a route and whether it follows a schedule (figure 5-1). Freewheeling services are those that do not follow a schedule, although they may follow a route, making them jitneys. Other freewheeling services follow neither schedule nor route. They operate at the margins of traditional transit and are particularly important in decentralized edge cities. With a nod to Joel Garreau, we call these services *edge transit*. Edge transit services most closely

FIGURE 5-1. *Typology of Urban Transportation Services*

	Route	No route
Scheduled	Scheduled bus services Deregulated British buses	
Nonscheduled (freewheeling)	Jitneys LDC jitneys Illegal jitneys in United States 1915 jitneys in United States Legal jitneys in United States	Edge transit Deregulated taxi services Illegal taxi services Commuter services Noncommuter shuttles

emulate the private automobile, but they are not in fact the focus of this book. This book pays due regard to this growing and important sector, but its core ideas pertain to route-based transit, both scheduled and freewheeling.

Chapter 5

Jitneys and Interloping

Jitneys are small, unscheduled vehicles plying a route. Americans today see little of them, but elsewhere, especially in less developed countries, people rely on them heavily. Jitneys often operate illegally, picking up passengers along the routes of scheduled bus service, a practice called "interloping." Whether jitneys are able to interlope depends critically on whether they are effectively prevented—not just by written law but also by actual enforcement—from pulling up to the curb at bus stops where passengers congregate. In other words, the viability of interloping depends on whether the scheduled bus services enjoy secured and exclusive *curb rights*. Jitneys are often regarded as the scabs of the transit world, but they have invariably offered consumers advantages in terms of lower charges and greater flexibility, frequency, and speed. So jitney interloping often survives, to the outrage of public transit agencies.

The U.S. Jitney Experience, 1914–16

At the turn of the twentieth century, horsecars and cable lines gave way to the new streetcars running on electricity. Streetcar technology brought a significant decrease in the cost of public transit and apparent economies of scale in service provision.[1] Across the United States, electric streetcar companies were given monopolies in the form of exclusive franchises to routes. In exchange for the monopoly right, the municipalities regulated the companies by fixing their fares, routes, and service levels.

In 1914, however, a decentralized form of transit emerged. Automobile owners used their cars to transport passengers for a "jitney," the slang term for a nickel. Jitneys offered the novelty of riding in an

1. Eckert and Hilton (1972, p. 295); Hilton (1985, p. 34).

33

automobile and traveled 150 to 200 percent faster than the streetcars. They were also more comfortable and less crowded. Mostly, the jitneys interloped along the streetcar routes, picking up passengers who were waiting for the streetcar. Drivers would occasionally deviate from the main route to drop off passengers. Jitneys quickly became popular, especially with people who put a high value on time. They rapidly spread throughout the nation. By 1915 there were 62,000 in operation nationally, and a trade journal, *The Jitney Bus*, was founded.[2]

Unlike electric streetcars, jitneys did not show economies of scale in the production cost of additional traveling capacity. As a result, their services were loosely organized and spontaneous. Most drivers were independent and worked part-time to supplement their income. Many were simply working people who picked up passengers on the way to their regular jobs.[3] There was a good deal of turnover among drivers each month.[4] Jitneys readily adapted to weather, time of day, day of the week, holidays, special events and other changing conditions that affected demand. Routes and the general supply of jitneys were highly flexible. Despite the decentralization of the service, an order of customs, voluntary associations, and company fleets evolved to meet institutional and market needs. These associations were formed to help drivers obtain insurance, share maintenance service, protect them from hostile legislation, and in some cases coordinate routes and schedules.[5]

The popularity of the jitneys undoubtedly affected the revenues of the electric streetcar companies. A few months after the introduction of jitney service in Los Angeles, for example, Los Angeles Railways was losing $600 a day, laying off employees, and cutting back on service.[6] Another report indicated that Los Angeles trolley companies were losing $3 million a year to jitneys, and Public Service of New Jersey reported an annual loss of $4 million to them.[7] In some smaller cities jitneys put streetcar companies out of business.[8]

2. Eckert and Hilton (1972, pp. 295–96); Rosenbloom (1972); Saltzman and Solomon (1973).

3. Eckert and Hilton (1972, p. 294).

4. Public Utilities Commission (California) (1918, p. 86).

5. Eckert and Hilton (1972, pp. 295–97).

6. Eckert and Hilton (1972, p. 295).

7. Rosenbloom (1972, pp. 5–6).

8. Saltzman and Solomon (1973, p. 63).

Jitneys no doubt skimmed some of the cream of the streetcar business, yet they also served more passengers than were lost from streetcars and filled important market niches. They were used mainly for short-distance trips and provided transportation to people who would otherwise not have been served by the streetcar companies. Although they charged no more than the streetcars, their gross revenue far exceeded the streetcars' loss of revenue.[9]

The electric streetcar companies considered jitney services an infringement on their monopoly right, and "instead of trying to compete by introducing better and more variegated public transportation services, the transit industry's response to recognized competition was to attempt to regulate the innovations out of existence."[10] Streetcar companies lobbied local and state government to regulate the jitneys. Municipalities went along with streetcar demands, in part because the companies provided them tax revenue and free movement of police and fire department personnel.[11] Municipalities began to require jitney drivers to obtain liability bonds ranging from $1,000 to $11,000 per vehicle and obtain franchise licenses similar to those awarded to the streetcars. These and other anti-jitney ordinances proved fatal. Jitneys disappeared after just two years of remarkable growth and experimentation.

The jitney episode was one of change and discovery in an otherwise heavily regulated and monopolized industry. Passengers saw the benefit they were getting and left the streetcars en masse to patronize the jitneys. As the jitney industry grew in size and importance, it began to organize to better serve the paying customer. However, the episode also gives credence to public choice economists' ideas that regulators respond not to the needs of the public, but to the industry they regulate.[12] Despite the jitney's popularity with paying customers, regulators chose to neglect the clear potential for public betterment in favor of a static and knowable order.

The jitney episode may seem like ancient history, but it is a landmark on the road Americans have traveled. As soon as the automobile appeared, freewheeling transit appeared. Also making its appearance was the fundamental property rights issue that has

9. Eckert and Hilton (1972, p. 296); Rosenbloom (1972, p. 5).
10. Saltzman and Solomon (1973, p. 64).
11. Hilton (1974, p. 37).
12. Tullock (1967); Stigler (1971).

persisted ever since: Is interloping on scheduled service a form of thievery or a form of competition? The answer of the authorities was thievery, plain and simple. The item being "stolen" was passengers congregated at the curb, and the criminal means was "trespass" on transit stops. Instead of developing a framework that would accommodate competitive coexistence, officials stamped out freewheeling transit in favor of large-scale monopoly. Now after generations of protection, monopoly transit is collapsing, again due to competition from the automobile, but this time it is because virtually everyone can afford to be his own jitney driver. Freewheeling transit is an idea whose time had come in 1914 and has never really gone.

Transit in the LDCs: Jitneys and Route Associations

Transit services similar to the 1914–16 jitney experience operate today on the streets of hundreds of cities throughout the less developed world. In reviewing transit in Southeast Asia, for example, Peter Rimmer has described service needs being "filled by a 'mosquito' fleet of microbuses and minibuses based on converted sedans, ex-troop vehicles, and motorcycles with pedicabs."[13] Isaac Takyi has reported on six cities in less developed countries: "The archetypical urban jitney system consists of a constellation of loosely regulated owner-operated collective vehicles following more or less fixed routes with some deviations as custom, traffic, and hour permit."[14] Although there are important differences between the LDCs and present-day America, the LDC transit experience affords valuable lessons for transit strategies anywhere.

We have said that America is undergoing edgification, that wealth and the private automobile are diffusing urban development and reducing the demand for public transit. In the LDCs, however, migration from traditional communities to urban centers is heavy, and the demand for urban transit increases each year.[15] Edgification is still generations away. In this regard, the LDC experience is more like America past than present, and more like urban America than edge city.

There is another fundamental difference between the LDCs and America. Although there are extensive black markets in America, the

13. Rimmer (1988, p. 188).
14. Takyi (1990, p. 170). See also Grava (1980, p. 279).
15. Hamer and Linn (1987, p. 1258ff).

rule of law remains intact to a far greater extent than in most LDCs.[16] The average American rarely turns to the underground economy to serve his or her needs. The average Peruvian or Filipino or Kenyan rarely turns to the above-ground economy. There is a paradox here: sometimes the most *dirigiste* economies show the most entrepreneurial and freewheeling markets.

As government regulations proliferate, the edicts as to what one can and cannot do with his or her own property become so tangled, ambiguous, and obtuse that governance begins to lose its meaning and authority. Government becomes increasingly arbitrary, incomprehensible, and ineffectual.[17] Citizens lose respect for law and begin to disregard it altogether. Black markets expand, corruption spreads, and the rule of law disintegrates. In his famous study of the economy of Lima, Hernando De Soto commented that "the existing legal system—red tape, the widespread mistreatment on waiting lines, the bribes, the rudeness—are a Kafkaesque trap which prevents . . . resources from being used efficiently."[18] In the face of this trap, however, there emerge extralegal practices that often displace government-made law. Because government law has strangled itself, monopoly by regulatory law is impossible, and the streets of many LDC cities display a de facto sort of free market transit.

In most of the LDC cities there are official bus services that receive subsidies. Many jitneys operate without authorization, and others have official recognition but disregard government regulations. The rivalry between the subsidized buses and the jitneys depends on their relative appeal and their access to waiting passengers. Isaac Takyi has described the jitney's appeal:

They charge relatively low fares and provide wide coverage across a city, often serving poor areas that get no other service. Their operations are flexible so they can add service at peak times and quickly cover new neighborhoods. Their small size and cheap labor enables them to profitably provide frequent service in smaller neighborhoods and along narrow streets, as well as work the main thoroughfares. With fewer passengers, they often make fewer stops and faster time.[19]

16. Tucker (1993).
17. Hayek (1944); Cooter (1996).
18. De Soto (1989, p. 234).
19. Takyi (1990, p. 171).

These advantages also marked the American jitneys of 1915, but in that case regulations were imposed to undercut their competitive advantage. In the LDCs, laws are sometimes passed to prevent jitneys from interloping on official service and from establishing competing routes, but often the laws are not enforced. Takyi has observed the "loss of passengers at transit stops to jitneys during lean as well as peak periods."[20] Written laws may address jitney safety, routes, and fares, but among the LDCs compliance with laws and the success of the jitney systems varies widely.

Usually jitneys are loosely regulated and operate with small regard for the law, often paying bribes to be left alone. As service develops on heavy urban routes, curbside conflicts and confusions occur. Any operator that attempts to establish scheduled service will face a problem: other operators will interlope by running slightly ahead of the scheduled service or lingering at the curb to fill up, disrupting traffic and taking ridership from the arriving scheduled vehicle.[21] Consumers may be reasonably well served, but problems of discoordination and lack of trust are often severe.

A common development is for the jitney operators to form a route association. These are informal organizations created to bring order and regularity to service by creating an extralegal system of norms and explicit rules. Route associations seem in large measure to govern transit services in Lima, Hong Kong, Istanbul, Buenos Aires, Manila, Calcutta, and Caracas.[22] The route association becomes a regulatory body, somewhat like government but more local and entrepreneurial. The association lays down rules against interloping and deviating from schedules.

Associations create order sufficient to control wasteful conflict, but they also tend to operate as cartels. They fix fares on the route, though these may vary with time of day. Most important, they limit market entry.[23] By enforcing these practices, the associations manage to function as monopolies.

Jitneys initially transgress the curb rights of the formal bus opera-

20. Takyi (1990, p. 175).
21. Roth and Shephard (1984, p. 4); Takyi (1990, pp. 167, 175); Diandas and Roth (1995, pp. 27–28).
22. Roth and Shephard (1984); De Soto (1989);Takyi (1990).
23. Grava (1980, p. 282); Roth and Shephard (1984, p. 42); De Soto (1989, p. 99); Cervero (1996, pp. 132, 149).

tors, yet in time they organize to establish curb rights for themselves. How, then, do they prevent interlopers from transgressing their rights? The main answer seems to be physical intimidation and strong-arm tactics. Gabriel Roth has noted that "the methods used by route associations to protect their territory can become criminal, unlawful, perhaps even homicidal," and Sigurd Grava has described route enforcement using means "considerably beyond the law" by "district strongmen . . . local bosses, criminal gangs, powerful families, brotherhoods of operators or otherwise legal associations."[24] As is common in black markets everywhere, outlaw entrepreneurs employ violence to maintain their territory. In Mexico City the associations chase illegal operators from members' routes; in Lima they appoint "dispatchers" to monitor compliance with rules, and they bribe the police to accost and harass "pirates" who are trying to invade their routes.[25] Thus law is being disintegrated and regenerated in a continuing cycle.

Once route associations have organized their operations, they often turn to the government for official recognition. Through a long effort of lobbying, bribery, petition gathering, and so on, the association may acquire official status and be granted permits or licenses. Along with official recognition, however, come political obligations and regulations. Colombo and Lima show cycles of transit governance: once the decentralized private operators gain official recognition they are hamstrung by regulation and suffer invasion by a new generation of interlopers. Without curb rights, established officially or otherwise, orderly scheduled service does not last.[26]

There is, however, one situation in which scheduled service is preserved even when interlopers may carry on unhindered. If it is subsidized enough to allow it to charge fares lower than the jitneys, riders might choose it, rejecting the offers of the speedier jitneys. In strong, or so-called thick, markets or at peak hours the scheduled buses might be filled to capacity; jitneys supplement the service by carrying the excess demand and those willing to pay for better service. This vision conforms to De Soto's remark that jitneys "concentrate their

---

24. Roth (1987, pp. 224–25); Grava (1980, p. 282).
25. Cervero (1996, p. 132); De Soto (1989, p. 102).
26. Diandas and Roth (1995); De Soto (1989).

services in popular areas, while the state corporation and other formal companies mostly serve traditional neighborhoods."[27] In thin markets, there may be no curb rights to speak of, but jitneys do not headrun (that is, run slightly ahead) on official scheduled service because they cannot compete with the subsidized fare levels.

The LDC transit experiences are varied, but some fascinating models present themselves. Two stand out, and they are distinguished mainly by the treatment of curb rights. First, during certain periods in thick markets, curb rights have been minimal and a cascade of jitneys serves people efficiently and reliably. Scheduled service that receives no subsidies is likely to be dissolved by competition from the speedier, lower-cost jitneys. There are many advantages of this type of flexible service, and on the whole the performance of the jitney is thought to be "very positive."[28] Second, the development of route associations shows that operators will organize to establish normal operating practice and property rights in routes, bringing more order to the market. Now scheduled service is protected from the cascade of interlopers. These associations resort, when necessary, to strong-arm tactics, but they offer an interesting model of organizations setting standards for the market based on excellent local knowledge. According to Gabriel Roth and Anthony Shephard, given the circumstances, route associations work well, "serving both the public and their members."[29]

If the associations create property rights for themselves, however, they do so in a way that gives them monopoly control of routes. The associations limit market entry on routes and enable the jitney operators to act as a cartel. Thus it is but one sort of arrangement of property rights for transit. A more refined system of property rights might permit greater entrepreneurship and active competition on a single route.[30] The route associations create property rights in routes; but we shall be arguing that property rights ought to be given a more refined base, namely, separate and individual curb zones along a single route.

27. De Soto (1989, p. 94).
28. Grava (1980, p. 287).
29. Roth and Shephard (1984, p. 42).
30. Diandas and Roth (1995).

Illegal Jitneys in the United States

Black market transit is not restricted to less developed countries. In most major American cities, illegal transit, especially by taxicab, is extensive. We reserve the name jitney for vehicles that follow a fixed route at least loosely and a schedule at most loosely, and pickups and discharges per request. In contrast, illegal taxi services mostly either respond to radio dispatch or pick up passengers at stands. Although jitney and taxi services are distinct, an entrepreneur can choose at any given time to work at either type. Illegal taxis have been called jitneys to distinguish them from legal taxicabs and to avoid the connotations of terms such "illegal," "unlawful," and so forth. Following Peter Suzuki, we instead call them "gypsy" cabs.[31] We use "jitney" and "gypsy cab" strictly to distinguish between the type of service offered. Gypsy cabs will be discussed in chapter 6.

People who ride illegal jitneys in the United States give a number of reasons for preferring them to the city buses.[32] By far the most often mentioned is that they are faster and even cheaper than the buses. They also provide a more comfortable ride, with no standing, and many riders enjoy having a driver that speaks their native language. Finally, many patrons say that riding jitneys is safer than riding the bus. Because jitneys come more often, people do not have to wait as long at the bus stop, where they fear getting mugged.[33] Also, jitney drivers will not pick up passengers who are drunk and disorderly or who otherwise pose a nuisance. Jitney riders, who are mostly minorities, appreciate being able to escape the forced association with all comers that a public bus entails. Although opponents of illegal operators often claim that they imperil safety or commit crimes against passengers, researchers usually conclude that "this warning is entirely unfounded."[34]

A sudden event, or shock, such as a transit strike can provide an impetus for jitneys to descend on transit routes and interlope at stops. The event signals to all jitney operators that they can expect a significant outbreak of jitneying. Law breaking becomes a focal point

31. Suzuki (1985).
32. This paragraph is drawn from news reports of jitney riders. See Garvin (1992); Machalaba (1991); Bonapace (1993); Fried (1994); Onishi (1994).
33. Levine and Wachs (1986).
34. Davis and Johnson (1984, p. 97).

among potential jitney operators. To persist once enforcement begins, interloping must expand to the point at which the individual illegal operator finds safety in numbers, like someone taking part in a riot. Illegal interloping never persists as an occasional or small-scale phenomenon: it persists as a significant force or it is wiped out by law enforcement. In most U. S. cities, either market conditions have not favored illegal jitneys or enforcement has been effective.[35] The two notable outbreaks of such jitneying have been in New York City and Miami.

Modern jitney operations in New York City were prompted by the transit strike in 1980. Jitneys emerged to provide local service and feeder service to the Long Island Rail Road station in Jamaica (southeast Queens): according to D. Boyle, "the jitneys thrived along busy bus routes . . . because of the high numbers of people congregated at bus stops along these routes."[36] Boyle also suggests that jitney service has developed especially in neighborhoods of Caribbean immigrants because those riders had become accustomed to relying on them in their native lands.

Although the strike has long been settled and regular bus service reinstated, enforcement against the jitneys has been only sporadic. They reached the point of self-sustained operation in 1980 and have established associations. The authorities face the dilemma of cracking down on services that are well regarded by customers and treated sympathetically by reporters and news commentators. The vans "siphon off our revenue," according to a Metropolitan Transit Authority spokesman; an MTA executive claimed that each year the jitneys were diverting $30 million in revenue from the system.[37] Transit police have been assigned to areas near bus stops to crack down on the interlopers. In 1992 the *New York Times* reported, "In the 18 months ended December 1991, a special task force issued 6,542 civil notices of violation against the vans and 11, 773 criminal summonses . . . [and made] 251 arrests."[38] Still, the vans are thought to be uncontrollable. A police officer remarks that two or three vans sail by

35. Boyle (1993, p. 1) states, "Transit and planning personnel in Chicago, Los Angeles, Atlanta, and Houston indicated that jitneys were not operating in any extensive or organized fashion in their cities."

36. Boyle (1993, p. 3).

37. Zimmerman (1992); Machalaba (1991).

38. Mitchell (1992).

for every one he tickets. Van drivers pay small regard to the summonses. In 1991 the *Wall Street Journal* noted that in a single year the van drivers had been assessed fines of more than $4 million, but the city collected only $150,000.[39] The possibility of setting off racial confrontations probably dampens official will to go beyond current enforcement measures, which amount to random delay and hassles for the drivers and their patrons.

To operate legally the vans would have to obtain special permits, buy a special insurance policy, and undergo safety inspections each year. Applicants would also have to demonstrate an unmet public need, and applications would be open to comment and protest by the Metropolitan Transit Authority and by private carriers. The vans could then pick up and discharge passengers only by appointment, and of course not use city bus stops.[40] Between 2,400 and 5,000 vans flout these laws.[41]

Miami's experience has been similar. Miami has had a history of legal jitney service, but a 1989 state law inadvertently opened opportunities for extensive jitneying. The law prohibited local governments from regulating passenger carriers engaged in intercity service. This loophole provided the type of sudden shock that gives rise to an outbreak of jitneying. There was a surge in jitney services crossing the city boundaries between Miami, Miami Beach, Hialeah, and Coral Gables. The surge came from both licensed certificate holders, who expanded their operations to new unlicensed routes, and newcomers, primarily Caribbean immigrants, operating entirely without authorization.[42] Although subsequent legislation changed the intercity proviso, the critical mass had gathered and the "riot" set in motion. The Metropolitan Dade Transit Agency had to deal with an extensive system of illegal service that had strong public support and a strong racial component. Surveys showed 55 to 60 percent of the jitney passengers most frequently spoke a language other than English (mainly Spanish), and 78 percent earned less $20,000 a year.[43]

Dade County officials stated that at their peak the illegal jitneys

39. Machalaba (1991).
40. Cervero (1996, p. 75).
41. Boyle (1993, p. 4).
42. Urban Mobility Corporation (1992).
43. Urban Mobility Corporation (1992).

skimmed the cream from the bus routes.[44] Only some of these patrons, however, were would-be transit riders: the jitneys thus developed new markets of their own. The Urban Mobility Corporation found that the jitney fleet of 400 vans carried about 45,000 riders each weekday, or about 20 percent of the number of weekday riders on the public transit system.[45] In surveys, 50 percent of jitney riders said that they "always ride the jitney," while 31 percent said they use "whichever vehicle arrives first." More than 30 percent said that if the jitneys were not available, they would travel by means other than the county transit system. The Urban Mobility Corporation estimates that 22 percent of the jitney riders were would-be riders of the public bus system.

After the Florida legislature had closed the loophole that had given rise to the jitney outbreak, enforcement had to be stepped up drastically to subdue it. In mid-1992 Dade County marshaled its resources and made enforcement of the law against jitneys a top priority. The county impounded more than 700 vehicles in 1992, playing the safety card to the press and the public. Jitney operations in Miami have returned to levels similar to those before the outbreak. Currently, thirteen companies operate legally on twenty-one routes. They are allowed to overlap their routes only 30 percent with public bus routes, so interloping is kept to a minimum.

The New York and Miami jitney experiences show again that unsubsidized private enterprise can supply fixed-route transit, even while having to cope with enforcement efforts directed against it. A critical variable in such experiences is whether scheduled services enjoy property rights in waiting passengers and the degree to which such rights are enforced.

Legal Jitneys in the United States

In a few places in the United States—most significantly Atlantic City, San Diego, Los Angeles, San Francisco, Houston, and Indianapolis—metropolitan authorities have allowed jitneys to operate legally. The success of these experiences has varied. Success or failure hinges upon issues of interloping and competition with subsidized buses.

44. Garvin (1992).
45. Urban Mobility Corporation (1992).

The sunny story has been Atlantic City, where jitneys were first seen in numbers in March 1915 at the height of a paralyzing trolley strike.[46] This, then, is another example of an unexpected shock giving rise to a jitney outbreak. Jitneys have flourished there ever since. Atlantic City is laid out along the coast, and a steady flow of jitneys, coming every five minutes, serves the main route paralleling the boardwalk and the casino strip.[47] Fully private and unsubsidized, the jitney system carries 11 million passengers a year (275 trips a year per capita). City officials also find that they have only a minimal need to oversee operations: a jitney association has evolved that very effectively manages service levels and polices driver behavior.[48]

Attempts to revive jitney service have been made in other cities. In 1979 San Diego deregulated jitneys. They quickly flourished, reaching a peak of about one hundred vehicles in 1984.[49] Jitneys were allowed to operate along bus routes but could not follow too closely behind scheduled buses and could not use public bus stops in the downtown area. But the jitneys began to interlope and cause congestion at bus stops. The city responded by excluding them from the airport and tourist areas, forbidding them to use the bus stops, and establishing special curbs, or holding areas, separate from bus stops, where they could pick up passengers. The idea of creating separate curb zones did not work. The combination of restrictions and a shrinking market at military facilities led to a deterioration of services. By 1996 only ten to fifteen operated, mostly serving passengers traveling to and from the Mexican border.[50]

Efforts to revive jitneys in other cities have not succeeded, but less because of regulation than subsidized competition. In Los Angeles in 1983 private jitneys were allowed to operate on thirty public transit routes. Matching the 85 cent public bus fare, they were initially successful, but they promptly withdrew once the city lowered bus fares to 50 cents.[51] In San Francisco more than one hundred jitneys survived from 1916 through the 1960s. By the 1970s, however, competition from subsidized buses and the new rail system undercut the

46. Cervero (1996, p. 48).
47. Heramb, Sen, and Sööt (1979).
48. Cervero (1996, pp. 52–53).
49. Reinke (1986, p. 9); Cervero (1996, p. 42).
50. Cervero (1996, p. 44).
51. Teal and Nemer (1986).

market. By 1996 only one route survived.[52] Similar stories may explain the demise of legal jitneying in Chicago and Ann Arbor.

Another reason jitney efforts may fail is simply that the market is too thin. In some cities they cannot compete with the private auto. This seems to have been the case in Houston and Indianapolis, where jitney services have been deregulated, but despite several attempts, no service has made a successful go of it.[53]

Jitneys have certain market advantages over scheduled bus service, but the experiences of legal jitneys in the United States demonstrated that the advantages are not always sufficient for survival. Subsidized bus fare may spell doom for jitney ridership. Interloping on scheduled bus services can lead to crackdowns. The inability to interlope or the lack of bus stops that serve as focal points where passengers can gather leaves a market in which the congregation of waiting passengers remains too thin. A sustainable market depends on some threshold number of passengers willing to wait for a cruising jitney, and of jitneys willing to cruise for passengers.

Conclusion

We have reviewed jitney experience in four contexts: the United States in 1914–16, the less developed countries, recent illegal markets in the United States, and recent legal markets in the United States. When jitneys have free run of the streets, they interlope at public transit stops. This represents a form of competition, but it is a form that is lawless. Various problems result. In the LDCs, jitney operators organize to manage the problems by forming associations. They create their own rules for the market, and the results are often comparatively good. But jitney associations also tend to operate as cartels, especially by limiting market entry.

The market advantages of jitneys are easy to see, yet their great potential continues to go untapped in the United States. If the problem of interloping and cartel behavior could be resolved, perhaps travelers could enjoy the blessings of both the freewheelers and scheduled service.

---

52. Cervero (1996, pp. 38–39).

53. Olsson and Kuzmyak (1985); Feldstein (1995); Urban Mobility Corporation (1992); Cervero (1996, p. 174ff).

Chapter 6

Edge Transit Services in the United States

U nder a regime of minimal regulation, transportation modes inevitably blend into one another: solo driving melds with carpooling, which melds with vanpooling, which melds with shuttle vans, which melds with shared-ride taxis, which melds with jitneys, which melds with minibuses, which melds with buses. The focus of this book is route-based transit, notably jitneys and buses, but a rounded discussion of transit policy needs to recognize the growing roles of transit services operating at the edges of route-based transit. Taxis (gypsy and legal), commuter services, and shuttles are the services that most closely approximate the private automobile, the giant of urban transportation.

Illegal Taxicabs

One pervasive form of illegal transit in America is the gypsy cab. Illegal cab services have developed primarily in low-income black neighborhoods, which are often poorly served by legal cab companies. Peter Suzuki has explained that, because these services are illegal and operate in neighborhoods that are predominately black, it is difficult for social researchers to do basic field work.[1] Suzuki overcame these barriers, worked as a gypsy driver in Omaha, and described the practices of the field. The cabs work the streets for hails, take telephone calls from nondescript stands, and cruise supermarket parking lots for shoppers who have arrived by bus but depart with groceries. These gypsy operators are often neighborhood features of

1. Suzuki (1985, p. 345).

long standing and do not compete directly with any lawful service. Compared with the jitney vans, illegal cabs enjoy a live-and-let-live attitude on the part of officials, but only as long as they do not become too ambitious or overtly commercial.

The situation in Pittsburgh has been studied by Otto Davis and Norman Johnson with the assistance of black students who worked their way into the network.[2] But little is known about the vernaculars of Baltimore, Boston, Chicago, Los Angeles, New York, Philadelphia, and elsewhere, and that which is known comes largely from the efforts of newspaper reporters.[3] Gypsy cabs are not confined to the United States; London alone supports a remarkable 40,000 illegal taxis.[4]

Even gypsy cabs need to be organized. Entrepreneurs run stands (or stations) where calls are taken and cabs dispatched. Suzuki described the illegal taxi stands of Omaha:

> The typical stand is an unkempt place, and many even have the doors and windows boarded up with plywood. The only indication that it is a stand may be a sign with the key words "delivery service," euphemism for jitney [that is, gypsy cab] stands. Inside a typical stand one sees a pool table or two and perhaps a soft-drink machine. Old wooden chairs and an old overstuffed sofa with its springs showing may also be found. Invariably, the stand will be dark and dingy, with only a naked light bulb or two lighting the interior. Even in the morning hours the stand may be a lively place, with drivers—usually males—shooting pool while waiting for the dispatcher's call.[5]

According to Davis and Johnson, stands are often found "near a bus stop, at the bottom of a steep hill, or near a shopping area." They emphasize that stand operators must protect their reputation for friendly, reliable, trustworthy service and screen drivers accordingly. Although outlaw existence might prevent them from investing in their place of business, they guard their brand-name capital. The gypsies also find their patrons by cruising the streets or arranging shared rides from the supermarket. They are cheaper than regular

2. Davis and Johnson (1984).
3. See the citations in Suzuki (1985, 1995).
4. Stevenson (1993).
5. Suzuki (1985, p. 342).

cabs, and tipping is not the custom. Forty percent of the drivers are part-timers, many being between jobs or driving as a second job. The full-timers "are often older persons, retired or disabled (almost always male), who have adopted this occupation as a means of supplementing other income (such as retirement pensions) or simply in order to have something useful to do."[6]

The relationship between gypsies and official cabs depends on particulars and history. Where gypsies hustle rides at the airport or cruise the territory of the legal cabs, as they do in New York, tension is severe and the authorities are more active in enforcement, mediation, and regulatory reform. Where gypsies function primarily in poor neighborhoods that are otherwise unserved, de facto accommodation typically is made by the official cabs and the authorities.[7] In Los Angeles in 1994 officials offered gypsy cabs license to operate legitimately, but only in the poor areas.[8]

The illegal jitneys and taxicabs can be said to confront a complex of economic and political factors. There are three variables that work together to determine the level of official restraint: the ire that the illegals arouse in legal operators, the political influence these competitors have with the authorities, and the will and ability of the authorities to police the illegals. If all three variables are strong, the illegals will be suppressed.

Illegal jitneys arouse tremendous ire when they travel the official bus routes and interlope at bus stops, and their bus competitors have much political muscle. For this reason such jitney operations are very rare in the United States. But in New York and Miami special circumstances and historical accident have generated a critical mass, and jitney operation has reached a scale such that the authorities lack the ability to shut them down. The political will comes to be influenced by public support for the illegals. As for gypsy cabs, they often exist simply because they do not arouse the ire of competitors. Whatever the calculus of power, once illegal operators become part of the status quo, it is difficult for the authorities to shut them down, because at bottom they are entrepreneurs peaceably offering a service to willing customers. As one Hispanic housewife, who rides illegal cabs

6. Davis and Johnson (1984, pp. 93, 97, 88).
7. Davis and Johnson (1984, p. 81).
8. Lacey (1994).

between Santa Ana and Tijuana, describes enforcement activities: "The ones who are bothering people are the police."[9] In time, illegal operators often obtain varying degrees of recognition de jure.

Taxi Deregulation

In our thinking, "transit" means nonautomobility, not nonautomobile, and taxis ought to be viewed as a prominent mode of transit. Taxis carry at least 40 percent more passengers nationwide than all other mass transit combined.[10] Taxis' share of total trips has remained steady while the bus and rail shares have shrunk. Taxi fares average five times more per passenger mile than fares of other transit services, so taxis must offer something that other transit modes do not.[11] They probably better serve emergency trips, the elderly and handicapped, business trips, and nighttime trips. Senior citizens, housewives, and the poor each account for a much higher share of taxi trips than their share of the population.[12]

That taxis have developed such a market share is remarkable in light of the constraints on their activities. Municipal (and sometimes state) authorities regulate them extensively, usually covering market entry, fares, service, and safety. The most obvious effect has been to reduce the number of taxis, restrict ridership, increase waiting time, and concentrate the number of firms in the industry.[13] Another effect has been to segment the market by race. Taxi drivers often refuse to serve minority areas of the city, and in consequence illegal taxis fill that niche.[14] Drivers also sometimes refuse short trips because regulated rates make them unremunerative. Finally, restrictions on shared rides decrease the occupancy rates and increase fares to the individual passengers.[15]

Taxi companies have not, however, been passive victims. Existing cab companies were the first to pressure municipalities to regulate the service.[16] Once entry restrictions were imposed, companies with

9. Gurza (1995).
10. Rosenbloom (1981); Wohl (1982, p. 329).
11. Wohl 1982, p. 329).
12. Weiner (1982, pp. 324, 327).
13. Rosenbloom (1981).
14. Suzuki (1985).
15. Frankena and Pautler (1986a).
16. Eckert (1970); Frankena and Pautler (1986b, p. 147).

permits enjoyed some monopoly power, with which they sought to increase fares and skimp on service. This led to a familiar dynamic of inducing further regulation to manage fares and service. The agencies charged with managing and enforcing the regulations operate according to their own peculiar logic, and consume resources in the process.[17] Leading taxi companies are now locked into a protected and highly regulated market and usually oppose any efforts to change the laws regulating the industry.

Economists have long argued that deregulation, especially of market entry, would allow the taxi market to expand. Public mobility would improve, entrepreneurs would differentiate services, fares would decrease, employment would increase, and perhaps with shared rides even congestion and pollution would decrease. Where deregulation has been carried out, some of the anticipated benefits have materialized. In San Diego, Seattle, Oakland, Fresno, Phoenix, Tucson, Sacramento, Kansas City, Tacoma, and Washington, the number of taxis increased greatly, the industry became much less concentrated, fares generally remained level, the average waiting time for a cab decreased, and the number of taxi trips per capita increased.[18] The magnitude of many of these changes, however, has been moderate.

On the whole, the effects of deregulation have been mixed. It seems to have led to declining incomes for taxi drivers.[19] Yet many people were able to earn incomes who could not before. Some researchers report improvements in service quality, while others report deteriorating quality and increased numbers of complaints.[20] In their lengthy review of taxi deregulation, Mark Frankena and Paul Pautler reported that across all deregulated cities there were as many cases of quality improvement as deterioration.[21]

Beginning in the 1970s a number of cities experimented with deregulation, but changes in the industry were disappointingly small. The apparent failures of deregulation were salient and well

17. Eckert (1970, 1973).

18. For increases in numbers, see Doxsey (1986); Teal and Berglund (1987). For fare levels, see Teal (1986); Styring (1994). See Frankena and Pautler (1986b, pp. 148ff) on all these points.

19. Duffy (1993); Teal and Berglund (1987).

20. Styring (1994) reports improvements. Duffy (1993); LaGasse (1986); and Teal (1986) report deterioration.

21. Frankena and Pautler (1986b, p. 151).

broadcast, and enthusiasm began to taper off. The recent taxi deregulations in Indianapolis, Denver, and Houston, however, indicate that some still believe in the benefits.

There are three reasons why deregulation has been regarded as a disappointment. First, analysts overestimated what would follow from deregulation because they did not recognize some of the inherent difficulties in the taxi market. Second, deregulation was usually incomplete and often poorly managed. Third, some of the benefits of deregulation are difficult to measure and have not been taken into account.

The taxi market involves problems in communication between customers and drivers or companies. Customers at the curb are uncertain about the terms offered by any particular cab and about alternative offers. These problems are inherently more severe for transit services than for most other consumer services. We shall take up this matter, especially in the context of taxi service at airports, in chapter 12.

Little entrepreneurial flair has been observed in cities that have deregulated.[22] Deregulation, however, has been only partial. Although most cities permitted free market entry, they did not fully deregulate fares and service. Shared-ride services generally remained forbidden. Yet shared-ride might be a valuable service at high-volume origins such as airports where an agent or stand operator helps passengers arrange shared rides. Shared-ride service is unlikely to develop in the absence of curbside coordinators or in dispersed origins and especially unlikely in edge cities where virtually everyone drives.[23] Another problem of incomplete deregulation has been in charging for short trips. In some deregulated cities taxis still could not price the short haul specially, so they continue to refuse such trips.[24]

There are some benefits from deregulation that have gone unnoticed, benefits associated with the changing status of cabs that were formerly illegal. Frankena and Pautler have argued that municipalities saved money by reducing the extent of regulations that they had to enforce. Sandra Rosenbloom said, however, that almost all cities had to spend more than before to track down independent and formerly illegal cabs and enforce safety codes.[25] The cost to municipalities is an empirical question, but we suspect that the cost of enforcing

22. Rosenbloom (1985, p. 191).
23. Teal (1986).
24. Frankena and Pautler (1986b, p. 155); Teal (1986).
25. Frankena and Pautler (1986b, p. 155); Rosenbloom (1986).

lighter regulations on a larger taxi market is less than the combined cost of enforcing heavier regulations on a smaller taxi market and of policing illegal cabs.

Peter Suzuki is the leading student of the illegal cab market, and points out that the deregulation literature has ignored the impact of erstwhile illegals.[26] Before deregulation, complaints about the illegals, which, like any black market service, probably had given ample cause for complaint, were not heard. With deregulation, large numbers of cabs suddenly entered the legitimate market, so the absolute number of complaints should have increased. Also, one would expect it to take some time for these taxis to bring themselves into compliance with safety and insurance codes.

Rosenbloom makes a telling point when she argues that the net benefits of taxi deregulation are diffuse and take time to accrue.[27] Deregulation has not been a dramatic success, but it is reasonable to maintain that it nets out as beneficial. Rosenbloom points out that it is difficult to sell taxi deregulation to politicians because it is asking them to risk conflict and turmoil today for modest benefits in the future. Perhaps taxi deregulation will become more palatable to officials as traditional public transit continues to decline, and if there is a general change in thinking about transit. If taxis come to be seen as part of transit's future, as belonging to the range of services between the private car and the city bus, policy reform for taxis might be undertaken in a new spirit.

Commuter Transit Services

Transit agencies have focused much of their efforts on serving commuters, particularly those traveling to downtowns. Yet traditional transit services face special problems in appealing to the commuter. (By "commuter" we mean someone who travels a considerable distance to work.) A commute on public transit generally involves numerous drawbacks, including walking to the stop, waiting, repeated stopping, and transferring. Public sector express services avoid some of these drawbacks, but they carry only a minute portion of total commuters. Since most commutes cross municipal boundaries, express commuter service depends on regional agency cooper-

26. Suzuki (1985, 1995).
27. Rosenbloom (1986).

ation, which may not be easy to achieve. Because gaps remain in the market, private commuter services have emerged.

Commuter transit services have distinguishing characteristics. First, most of the journey is an uninterrupted haul between the local neighborhood and the work center. At the home end of the main haul there might be either a small-radius scooping of passengers or a pick-up-and-discharge point, like a park-and-ride lot. Second, commuter trips are repeated week in and week out, and most commuters find that it makes sense to arrange for regular riding. Third, commuter transit services experience a downtime of several hours between the morning and evening rushes. In this section we will discuss the various types of private commuter transit services.

Figure 6-1 offers a typology of commuter transit. The top and bottom halves of the figure separate the alternatives by how the rider chooses to participate. The top half includes services for which the rider participates by the trip; no long-term commitment is required. The bottom half includes services for which the rider makes a longer commitment, usually by the month. The left and right sides divide services by whether the driver of the vehicle is a commuter or a commercial driver.

One of the significant advantages of having a commuter driver is that such services, including carpools and vanpools, avoid the taxes and regulations that pertain to income and labor, whereas using a commercial driver means taxes and regulation. Also, having a commuter driver eliminates the problem of driver downtime between morning and evening rush hours. The most spontaneous commuter-driver arrangement falls in the top-left cell. Advanced public transportation systems, or APTS, an idea studied and advocated by Melvin Webber and Robert Cervero, is a concept of commuter ride matching in real time.[28] The service would link in minutes persons offering a ride with persons seeking a ride. In other words, it arranges one-time, short-notice carpools.[29] A localized, low-technology variant exists in the San Francisco area. Cervero describes how on-the-spot carpools have developed at park-and-ride lots and elsewhere on the east side

28. Webber (1994); Cervero (1996, chap. 9).

29. The system would require some way of ensuring an acceptable level of personal safety for riders and drivers to overcome the natural concern about strangers. Webber suggests that if people are from the same neighborhood, safety is usually not a problem.

FIGURE 6-1. *Typology of Private Commuter Transit Services*

	Commuter driver	Commercial driver
Passenger participates by the trip	Advanced public transportation systems (APTS or on-the-spot carpools)	Commuter van Commuter bus
Passenger participates by the month (subscription or weekly or monthly pass)	Carpool Vanpool Buspool	Subscription van

of the Bay.[30] Drivers participate in order to cross the toll bridges in the free HOV lanes. Passengers get a ride into the city. Arrangements take place on the spot.

At the bottom left of figure 6-1 are the various kinds of pools. Carpools are by far the most significant form of commuter transit. They are often informal arrangements, but they are also encouraged, brokered, and even subsidized by employers. Commercial involvement in carpools is usually limited to ride-matching services. Public sector involvement takes the form of public park-and-ride lots, HOV lanes, ride-matching services, and marketing and publicity for ride sharing, as well as transportation demand management measures to discourage solo driving.

Vanpools are often employer sponsored and subsidized, but another form of vanpool has become increasingly popular. Vanpool-lease operators, such as Van Pool Services, Inc., and the Ford Corporation, provide organizational and insurance assistance and lease vans to individuals who want to vanpool.[31] Except for regular carpools, vanpools are the predominant form of unsubsidized, private commuter service.[32]

30. Cervero (1996, p. 97).
31. Kirby and others (1974, p. 234); Transportation Systems Center (1982, p. 313).
32. Giuliano and Teal (1985).

Even buses are used in commuter-driver arrangements. Buspool services tend to be much less expensive than subscription buses with commercial drivers. They usually use older buses and offer few amenities.[33] Extensive buspool operations have existed in Los Angeles and Virginia.[34] As of 1985 in Los Angeles they were regulated by the state Public Utilities Commission, which gave buspool lease companies monopoly privileges over specific routes. These companies primarily serve white-collar workers living at least twenty-five miles from downtown. In Virginia, buspools are not regulated, and firm size ranges from two to thirty-two buses. They serve mostly blue-collar workers and naval personnel in Newport News and Norfolk.

The services on the right side of figure 6-1 are less sharply divided between top and bottom: many commercial commuter services offer riders the choice of riding for a single day or of purchasing a monthly pass or subscription. Commuter van and bus services are often developed for specific destinations or groups of riders. They are usually organized by employers or employees, but sometimes by transit entrepreneurs. In 1974 Ronald Kirby and his colleagues described subscription bus operations in St. Louis, Illinois, Michigan, Virginia, San Francisco, Los Angeles, and Washington, D. C.[35] The services varied somewhat, but they shared some general characteristics. They often recruited riders at large employment centers to assist in building a subscription bus route, and usually served only markets with a very long haul. They required a minimum threshold of committed subscription riders, but sometimes would take additional riders on a per-trip basis. One bus service in Los Angeles simply facilitated commuter organization of the route and then provided the bus and driver.[36]

Private commuter van service has developed in many places where either regulation prevents larger bus operations or market conditions cannot support larger vehicles. Commuter vans are particularly prevalent in New York City, where they are technically illegal, but encounter little enforcement. Jay Walder described commuter van operations:

33. Teal and others (1984, p. 63).
34. Giuliano and Teal (1985).
35. Kirby and others (1974, pp. 236–48).
36. Transportation Systems Center (1982, p. 315).

The vans typically seat eleven to fifteen passengers, operate during rush hours, and charge the same fare as authorized express buses. Beyond these generalizations, individual arrangements may vary widely. The van operator may park and work in Manhattan, ride around until the afternoon trips, or return to Staten Island after the morning runs. The operator may make one or more trips per day. Passengers may ride regularly or sporadically, they may be friendly or strangers. Pickups may be at homes, street corners, or bus stops. Payment may be made on a daily or weekly basis.[37]

Flexibility allows the vans to offer superior service at the same price as public express buses. In fact, the Congressional Budget Office found that legal commuter vans operate at about one-third the cost of public buses per passenger mile.[38] About 74 percent of riders of the vans described by Walder formerly rode the public buses. Evidently the passengers find the service sufficiently appealing to make up for the transaction costs associated with unauthorized, loosely structured service. In addition, the vans make a profit, while the public express buses operated at a loss (and according to Walder would do so even if they had the passengers that are carried by the vans). Commuter vans operate similarly in Miami, but are more actively suppressed by the authorities.[39] If policymakers were to remove regulatory barriers and to implement HOV lanes or road pricing, commuter van services could be much more competitive with the private auto and might proliferate.[40]

Regulation of commercial commuter services varies from state to state. The most common restriction is that a proposed service must show a "public need" to obtain permission to operate. Regulators generally interpret this in the following way: if a route or market is served by public transit, there is no public need for a private service. Thus private service is prevented from competing with public service. Regulators often require excessive insurance. In addition, many jurisdictions do not allow private transportation services to use owner-drivers. They require companies to use employees who are paid wages or salaries and receive all mandated benefits, such as

37. Walder (1985, 105ff).
38. Congressional Budget Office (1988, p. 35).
39. Gómez-Ibáñez and Meyer (1993, p. 5ff).
40. Poole and Griffin (1994).

workman's compensation. Companies typically would prefer to use owner-drivers, not only to avoid workman's compensation, labor and customer litigation, and social security taxes, but also because doing so creates better incentives for hard work, safety, and vehicle maintenance. What is more, entrepreneurs are wary of regulator caprice, and for good reason.[41] The burden of regulations certainly diminishes the private provision of commuter services. As a result, there are more commercial commuter operations where regulation is light or where firms can secure franchises to specific markets.

Kirby and his colleagues identified three market characteristics for successful commuter transit service: long trips, which make service a closer substitute for the automobile, a large concentration of employment in a small area, and socioeconomic homogeneity within the potential market.[42] Congested highway access and high parking costs can also be important.[43] Citing the experience of a successful subscription bus service in southern California, Transportation Systems Center said a service should have between three and five stops, travel a direct route, pick up most people at the last origin, and drop off most people at the first destination.[44] Furthermore, if road pricing were also to exist, the cost of solo driving would increase and commuter transit would be made significantly more competitive with the private auto.

Noncommuter Door-to-Door Services

Noncommuter, shared-ride door-to-door services are generally summoned by phone or arranged on a subscription basis. They take a variety of forms, notably dial-a-ride, shared-ride taxis, and shuttle

41. Two recent examples from southern California show how justified these fears are. The Prime Time airport shuttle company has been continually harassed and prosecuted by the Public Utilities Commission (PUC) for using owner-drivers, even though airport and state regulations read as though such practice is permitted. Many other firms use owner-drivers as well, but the PUC appears to be singling out Prime Time. After spending nearly $1 million in legal fees, Prime Time won its battle against the PUC. Second, Young (1995) describes how the PUC is considering changing regulations governing what it calls "tot toters," or private transporters of young children. It is unclear why the PUC feels that it must change the regulation of existing providers just because the practice is expanding.

42. Kirby and others (1974, p. 248ff).

43. Giuliano and Teal (1985).

44. Transportation Systems Center (1982).

vans. Small niche markets call out for these types of services, but state regulations commonly obstruct entrepreneurial response to such opportunities.

In spite of obstructions, private providers have gained footholds in some markets. On a small scale, shuttle services are provided by unsubsidized private companies, senior citizens' organizations, charitable organizations, and employer associations.[45] There has also been enormous growth in private shuttle van companies offering services for children going to sports practice, music lessons, and so forth.[46] Cervero reports that there are 250 firms in forty-three states offering child van services.[47] Many are one- or two-van operations, but Kids Kabs has franchised operators in seven states. A trade association called the National Child Transportation Association has formed. The operators exploit flexibility by providing transportation to seniors and to teenagers and even by delivering packages.

While private providers of noncommuter services struggle with regulatory burdens, public transit agencies remain focused on serving commuters and cannot bother with niche markets. In response to extensive lobbying, some public transit agencies offer limited dial-a-ride services. These are door-to-door services offered primarily to those such as the elderly, the handicapped, and children who have difficulty using regular transit service. The service quality is not as high as a private taxi, since the ride is shared, but it is cheaper.

Some public transit agencies operate their own dial-a-ride vans or buses, but more commonly they contract with a taxi company to provide subsidized service.[48] This is particularly telling because it demonstrates the appropriateness of private service in these markets. Dial-a-ride service is essentially a shared-ride taxi, summoned by

45. Transportation Systems Center (1982, p. 306).
46. Gardner (1994).
47. Cervero (1996, pp. 87ff).
48. Becker and Echols (1983, p. 56) pointed out the difficulties that public transit providers have in accepting the use of these edge types of services. First, the services are usually new and innovative, threatening the status quo. Second, public transit labor resists their introduction as constituting a threat to jobs. In addition, taxi companies and other potential providers resist schemes so as to have the services contracted to themselves. They see subsidized services as competition even though they will be the ones providing the services. Perhaps they are taking a long-term view and do not want alternative services to get a foothold.

phone and publicly subsidized. Commercial vehicles devoted to dial-a-ride service may not be used for other types of service. The service is provided at lower cost by private firms under contract than by public transit agencies. However, publicly operated dial-a-ride vans have higher productivity than contract taxi companies.[49]

Public transit agencies have difficulty accepting the use of these edge-type services.[50] First, the services tend to be new and innovative, threatening the status quo. Second, public transit workers resist these services as threats to their jobs. In addition, potential providers such as taxi companies resist schemes to have the services contracted to themselves. They see the services as competition even though they will be the ones providing it. Perhaps they are taking a long-term view and do not want such alternative services to get a foothold.[51]

Even without public subsidies, private firms have succeeded in providing dial-a-ride service, sometimes with a municipal franchise and sometimes with no public sector involvement at all.[52] The keys to such success are that the competition from subsidized public service must be weak and shared-ride service must be legally permitted. There are few urban areas where these two conditions are met.

The experience of airport shuttles offers valuable lessons. When heading to the airport, the shuttle vans may pick up at hotels or by prearrangement only, not by street hails. Most firms use dispatchers to arrange shared-ride journeys on short notice. For the trip originating at the airport, the vans must pick up only at designated curb spaces. Two types of curb arrangements exist. At the Los Angeles airport, until recently, shuttle curbspace was open to all shuttle companies. It was a commons. As a result, even when a customer called one shuttle company for pickup, he often got aboard whichever one came first. This form of interloping caused waste and uncertainty. Because many of the interlopers or transient operators offer much lower quality service, customers are often soured on shuttle vans in general. SuperShuttle, the largest shuttle company in Los Angeles, claims that after curb space was made a commons, the shuttle busi-

49. Teal, Marks, and Goodhue (1979, p. 2); Teal (1988, p. 218). Teal and others (1984, p. 17) credit the higher productivity to more effective dispatching, resulting in a greater number of shared rides.
50. Becker and Echols (1983, p. 56).
51. Teal, Marks, and Goodhue (1979, p. 2).
52. Kirby and others (1974); O'Leary (1982); Transportation Systems Center (1982).

ness in general declined. The company has been successfully operating its own vans elsewhere around the country but has stopped operations in Los Angeles and merely franchises its name. SuperShuttle's complaints about curbside conflict have been substantiated and remedied by recent changes at the airport. In 1994 Los Angeles International assumed staging responsibilities by assigning a person at each shuttle curb to coordinate passengers and vans. This has significantly reduced interloping and related problems.[53]

Most other airports allot each shuttle company exclusive curb space to pick up passengers. Firms are able to cultivate brand-name recognition, and service quality may provide a competitive edge. SuperShuttle claims that at airports with curb rights, the shuttle van market has been steadily expanding. Again, the lesson appears to be the judicious use of private curb rights to give foundation to a self-forming order.

Although public transit is usually thought of as route-based services, edge transit services—taxis, commuter services, and shuttles—are also a large and growing part of the transit system, often complementing route-based service. Private, unsubsidized provision of edge transit service has proved itself in many isolated cases. Regulatory barriers, competition from subsidized public services, and free highway access for the solo driver have hampered the market development of these services. If the government wants to increase vehicle ridership or make transit available for equity reasons, the best plan would be a system of rider subsidies or vouchers for taking buses, shuttles, or shared-ride taxis.[54] Such a system would be rich in flexibility and entrepreneurial discovery and would be self-correcting by virtue of competitive market forces.

53. The information on SuperShuttle comes from interviews with Mitchell Rouse, the CEO of SuperShuttle. Information about recent changes in airport practice comes from interviews with a shuttle curb coordinator and shuttle van drivers. This information is congruent with the discussion in Cervero (1996, p. 191ff).

54. User-side subsidies, like food stamps or school vouchers, allow government to subsidize certain riders while leaving the market to discover and operate efficient means of producing transportation. Kirby (1982) surveyed a number of user-side subsidy programs, finding that they have been cost effective and show little fraud.

Chapter 7

Bus Privatization and Deregulation in Britain

During the 1980s, in one of the most significant events ever in transportation policymaking, Britain privatized and deregulated almost all bus services except those in London. Scholars and government officials alike have anticipated, debated, scrutinized, and reviewed the results to a degree that is both remarkable and exemplary. Before deregulation, opponents focused on integrated planning, coordinated systems, and economies of density in arguing for the retention of some level of central planning.[1] Supporters of deregulation discounted these arguments and invoked basic market principles, maintaining that free enterprise could do for bus transport what it had done for other services.[2] As it turns out, the deregulated bus industry has evolved in ways that surprised both camps. It has experienced reduced load factors, little fare competition, little on-the-road competition, and considerable market concentration.

Background to Deregulation and Privatization in Britain

Britain had a competitive and expanding private bus industry until 1930, when the government passed the Road Traffic Act, imposing a system of regulations that converted the bus industry into segmented local monopolies. By the early 1980s, buses carried one-fifth the share of travelers they had carried at their peak.[3] The government decided that public spending on bus transit had to be reduced drasti-

1. Gwilliam, Nash, and Mackie (1985a, b); Savage (1986a).
2. Beesley and Glaister (1985a, b).
3. Banister (1985, p. 99).

cally, and in 1984 it published a white paper calling for privatization and competition.[4]

The white paper anticipated that privatization and competition would result in lower fares, lower costs of operation, better service, increased patronage, and new operators. It also suggested that some "socially necessary" services might still require subsidy, but that these services be provided privately under competitively tendered contracts. The government would mainly enforce safety regulation and adherence to registered routes.

These proposals sparked heated debate. A series of articles, pro and con, appeared in *Transport Reviews* in 1985.[5] Table 7-1 summarizes the predictions from both camps. Opponents of deregulation believed that a gradual approach, retaining some central planning, was better than a precipitous one. They argued that competitive contracting for bus services, creating competition *for* the market rather than *in* the market, would capture most of the benefits and none of the disorder of full deregulation. Retaining some central control would allow authorities to avoid undesirable outcomes and use bus services as a policy tool for various social goals. Supporters of deregulation contended that the supposed "disorder of deregulation" was simply planner's angst over loss of control and that only full deregulation would permit the industry to cope with declining patronage and subsidies. They recognized that profound changes in the industry would be required, which would not likely come from continued central planning. They also pointed out that the regulator, lacking local knowledge, has great difficulty in identifying good and bad outcomes, whereas profits in a competitive market give entrepreneurs clear feedback on their decisions.

The 1985 Transport Act took two major steps for all bus markets, except in London.[6] (In London competition is required only as competitive contracting; there is no on-the-road competition.) First, the act privatized: it reorganized publicly owned bus lines into private companies. Second, it deregulated, but deregulated in one of a number of possible manners. Specifically, the act required operators

4. Banister (1985); Savage (1993); Hibbs (1993).

5. Gwilliam, Nash, and Mackie (1985a, 1985b); Beesley and Glaister (1985a, 1985b); Foster (1985).

6. Gómez-Ibáñez and Meyer (1990); Banister and Pickup (1990); White (1995).

TABLE 7-1. *Predictions and Outcomes of Bus Privatization and Deregulation in Britain*

| Subject | Predictions regarding bus deregulation | | Outcomes |
	Against deregulation	For deregulation	
Competition	Deregulation will not lead to a contestable market since there are sunk costs for new operators and incumbent operators have an advantage over new entrants	Deregulation will lead to a contestable market as new operators are free to enter and the law ensures they will be able to compete on equal terms	Some on-the-road competition occurs, but contestability limited by schedule jockeying, forty-two-day wait period, and sunk costs
Costs	There is some scope for cost savings, but deregulation is not necessary to achieve them. Under deregulation, most of the savings will be realized by cutting wages, to the detriment of bus employees	Competition will lead to cost savings of up to 30 percent. While wages will probably be cut, the industry will employ more people	Operating costs fell by 40 percent per bus-kilometer. Cost savings were achieved by cutting wages and employment
Fares	Because of elimination of cross-subsidy, fares will rise on many routes	Competitive pressure will force fares down on many routes	Fares increased 17 percent between 1987 and 1994
Congestion	Congestion will be a problem as number of buses increases	Congestion problems will be limited and local, and the law makes provisions for alleviating problems that arise	No evidence of any significant congestion problems associated with buses
Service	Because of elimination of cross-subsidy, service levels will fall for late nights, weekends, and in peripheral locations. Reliability of service will decline due to congestion increasing	Local government can maintain service levels by competitively tendered contract. Operators have every incentive to maintain reliable service, and the government has power to enforce adherence to posted schedules	Service levels, as measured by bus-kilometers, rose by 17 percent after deregulation. Some reductions in weekend and late-night service occurred

Innovation	Innovation is sufficient in a regulated environment	Deregulation will lead to greater innovation and responsiveness to customers	Significant successful innovation has occurred, particularly the widespread use of minibuses
Patronage	Higher fares, reduced service, unreliability, and instability will lead to a decline in patronage	Lower fares and improved service will increase patronage on some routes	Patronage fell precisely the amount that would be expected, taking into account the long-term ridership trend and the increase in fares
Integration	Operators will have no incentive to integrate services. This will reduce service quality and access	Operators will have an incentive to integrate services if passengers want it	Interoperator trips more expensive and difficult than before, but still a small share of all trips
Safety	Safety will decline as congestion increases, vehicles deteriorate, and staff training falls off	Existing regulations provide for adequate safety enforcement	No decrease in industry safety, despite increase in bus age and decrease in maintenance staff
Costs of regulation	Capture of regulatory bodies is not a problem, nor are the costs of administering a competitive contract system	The administrative costs of regulation are high, as are those of a competitive contract system. Capture of regulatory bodies is a constant risk with regulation	Government expenditures on the bus industry fell by over 50 percent, or nearly £250 million

to register the commencement of, or changes to, scheduled bus service at least forty-two days in advance of the change. Thus free-wheeling jitneying was not permitted. Furthermore, the act required that any operator be permitted to set up and register any schedule, *making use of the bus stops regardless of the comings and goings of other scheduled services.* The only grounds for local government to refuse to allow a service was serious safety or traffic congestion problems. Besides privately registered routes, local authorities could supplement services by putting unserved routes out for competitive tender.

Costs, Public Subsidy, Service Changes, and Innovation

As both sides predicted, privatization unequivocally lowered the operating costs of the industry (table 7-1). By 1993 the cost reduction per bus-kilometer within the industry overall was around 40 percent. Companies realized reductions mainly by reducing wages and employment and increasing productivity.[7] Many new bus drivers were willing to work for wages less than what the public transit union had been demanding. Former public firms found plenty of deadwood in their supervisory staffs and also discovered that they could maintain the buses adequately with fewer maintenance workers. These changes had no effect on the safety of the industry.[8] As a result, by 1994 total employment in the industry had decreased 15 percent, but labor productivity had risen 42 percent.

The government now spent much less on the bus industry. By 1991 support had fallen by more than 50 percent, almost 250 million pounds.[9] But even though costs had been greatly reduced, the reduction in government subsidization meant fares would increase. Fares were also driven upward by an expansion of service on new and lightly traveled routes. The increases in levels of service surprised many observers. Passengers did not have to travel as far to the nearest bus stop. In addition, the need to change buses for various origins and destinations was reduced.[10]

7. Banister and Pickup (1990, p. 80); White (1995, p. 194); Mackie, Preston, and Nash (1995, p. 238).
8. Savage (1993, p. 153); White (1995, p. 190).
9. White (1992, p. 50).
10. Banister and Pickup (1990, p. 74).

The quest for profits motivated the industry to adopt a number of innovations, the most significant being the introduction of minibuses.[11] These enabled the companies to increase service levels, reduce operating costs, and increase productivity (the ratio of passenger miles to costs). Several studies had suggested that minibuses presented an opportunity for service gains, but only the competitive pressure of deregulation moved the companies to adopt them.[12]

Competition and Contestability

The opportunities afforded bus companies by the reforms led to two changes in the industry that had not been predicted. The first was the manner in which firms competed, and the second was the steady tendency toward market concentration into fewer and fewer firms. Economists have not offered a complete explanation for these developments, nor have they discussed alternative forms of deregulation (aside from competitive contracting). But both changes can be explained largely by the specific form the British deregulation took.

Although on-the-road competition was initially strong, it has tapered off to a level that is less than was expected by supporters of deregulation, but perhaps more than expected by opponents.[13] Participants in the debate over privatization, however, focused less on competition on the road than on contestability, the ability of potential market entrants to discipline incumbent firms. In the simple picture of contestability, potential entrants discipline incumbents by being ready to make superior service or price offers to consumers, who in that event choose the entrant rather than the incumbent.

There are a number of indications that contestability has been somewhat effective in the privatized British bus market. Direct competition on many routes and the use of defensive measures by incumbent firms to fend off competition indicate that entry influences the incumbent.[14] There is a steady, if small, flow of new entrants into the market.[15] And the profits of bus firms were small in the first two

---

11. Gómez-Ibáñez and Meyer (1990, p. 15); Banister and Pickup (1990, p. 73); Mackie, Preston, and Nash (1995, p. 234).

12. Walters (1979); Bly and Oldfield (1986).

13. Dodgson (1991, p. 125); Hibbs (1993, p. 52).

14. Banister and Pickup (1990, p. 72); Gómez-Ibáñez and Meyer (1990, p. 11).

15. Mackie, Preston, and Nash (1995, p. 241).

years after deregulation.[16] One might expect that if the market were not very contestable, incumbents would enjoy some monopoly power and higher profits.

But other observers present a more pessimistic view on contestability.[17] They contend that because direct competition in the bus market is not widespread and constant, contestability has been imperfect. Contestability may thus be constrained by the sunk costs of establishing a scheduled service and the economies of experience held by incumbent operators. Another constraint of contestability, which they do not mention, is the ability of an incumbent firm to react quickly to a competitive challenge. Contestability theory suggests that if an incumbent firm can quickly and easily reduce its fares when a competitor challenges it, would-be entrants might be reluctant to enter, even in a market with high fares.[18] The challenger can no longer expect to grab market share by offering a lower price, and the incumbent has the advantage of experience, reputation, and, in most cases, size.

In fact, it has been very rare in the British experience for companies to compete by offering lower fares.[19] Rather, real bus fares increased 17 percent between 1986 and 1994.[20] Instead of lower fares, companies chose to offer more frequent service than their competitors. Price cutting does not necessarily result from free competition, as has been learned from the experience of deregulated taxi markets.[21] It seems that information and coordination problems between drivers and potential riders may push transit markets toward a single, or focal, rate of fare. People do not necessarily make a committed choice between two carriers; often they merely go to the curb and catch the first one that comes by.

Although a clear picture of competition in the bus industry is difficult to draw, it is easier to see the increasing concentration in the industry. There has been a wave of mergers between large incumbent firms and small rivals and many mergers between firms that do not

16. White (1992, p. 51); Gómez-Ibáñez and Meyer (1990, p. 17).

17. Mackie, Preston, and Nash (1995, p. 232); Dodgson and Katsoulacos (1991, pp. 265–66).

18. Bailey (1981); Bailey and Friedlaender (1982); Armstrong, Cowan, and Vickers (1994).

19. Dodgson and Katsoulacos (1991, pp. 271–72).

20. White (1995, p. 198).

21. Frankena and Pautler (1986a); Teal and Berglund (1987).

directly compete against each other.[22] These mergers have often been in the form of holding companies with geographic dispersion of subsidiaries.[23]

The result has been concern about industry concentration and a plethora of explanations for its development: economies of scope and management efficiencies; and financial advantages of larger firms, managerial economies of scale, and purchasing power.[24] Holding companies may offer such advantages as very low costs and the ability to move vehicles and managers from subsidiary to subsidiary as market conditions dictate.[25] Firms with large networks also have a distinct advantage in the growing use of single-rate unlimited-travel fare cards. Larger firms enjoy considerable economies of scope in scheduling buses and avoiding long layovers between runs.[26] The managers of formerly public firms may have retained their old habits of output maximization, even though they are inappropriate for the new goal of profit maximization.[27] The issue of integration calls to mind yet another explanation: there has been a steady decline in interoperator ticket availability. In one case the removal of schedule coordination and interoperator ticketing led to a 20 percent reduction in ridership.[28]

Schedule Jockeying and Route Swamping

Although there are detailed reports of the outcomes of deregulation, there have been few attempts to explain it, and even the reports overlook a fundamental issue: whether an operator is able to appropriate its investment in generating passenger congregations at the curb. The disappointing lack of competition in fares and service quality, and the increase in industry concentration, makes sense when one thinks of firms seeking to secure their claim to waiting passengers. British bus deregulation is another story of deficient curb rights.

22. Savage (1993, p. 147); Mackie, Preston, and Nash (1995, p. 235).
23. Gómez-Ibáñez and Meyer (1990, pp. 12–13).
24. Hibbs (1991, p. 4); Mackie, Preston, and Nash (1995, pp. 235–36); White (1995, pp. 202–03).
25. Gómez-Ibáñez and Meyer (1990, pp. 12–13).
26. Nash (1988, p. 110).
27. Dodgson and Katsoulacos (1991, p. 267).
28. Dodgson (1991, p. 124); Nash (1988); White (1992, p. 56).

Under the reforms, registering a scheduled service does not secure a company a right to the passengers congregating at the curb. A company running scheduled service is assured that it will not encounter any interloping by unscheduled carriers, but it may well encounter interloping by scheduled carriers who register their own service to arrive just moments before the service of the first firm. The law does not proscribe this, and local authorities are obliged to allow it. Many British bus operators avail themselves of this strategy, which we call *schedule jockeying*.[29] Because the established firm has no window of security from the schedules of competitors, passengers waiting at the curb can be snatched up by competitors offering comparable fares.

Incumbent bus companies, however, quickly learned to monitor the registration of new services by competitors using this strategy and often respond in kind. The forty-two-day registration period makes it easy for companies to see each other's changes in service and to respond in a potentially endless regress. John Dodgson and Y. Katsoulacos have described a typical conflict between an incumbent bus firm, Little Gem, and an entrant firm, Bee Line: "[Bee Line] started operating in South Manchester with a fleet of minibuses which soon totaled 225 vehicles. The entrant charged the same fare scale as Little Gem. [The incumbent's] response was to match the entrant's services with its own fleet of minibuses . . . operating along very similar routes."[30]

In the face of this prospect of mutually destructive battle, the incumbent has often responded simply by scheduling service so frequently that the challenger cannot expect to get enough riders to make a go of it. This practice, known as *route swamping*, has been very common.[31] Incumbent firms have an investment in the passengers waiting at the curb; the service they have been providing is what draws the passengers there. Faced with interlopers engaged in schedule jockeying, they turn to route swamping simply as a means of protecting their investment. Route swamping has a twofold strategic quality: it not only drives out the current challenger, it also discour-

29. Dodgson (199, p. 126); Savage (1993, p. 146); Gómez-Ibáñez and Meyer (1990, p. 13).

30. Dodgson and Katsoulacos (1991, p. 269).

31. Gómez-Ibáñez and Meyer (1990, p. 13); Dodgson (1991, p. 126); Dodgson and Katsoulacos (1991, p. 269); Savage (1993, p. 146).

ages future challenges. Larger incumbent firms have been known to maintain "fighting fleets" that were "available immediately to meet any competitive challenge."[32] The ability of incumbent firms, by virtue of the forty-two-day registration period, to change their schedules quickly and easily in reaction to entry constrains contestability in the same way that easy and quick adjustment of prices does in standard contestability theory.

Under the British deregulation, an incumbent will find it worthwhile to invest in attracting passengers out to the curb only if it can secure its claim to those passengers, and it can do this only if it can fend off the schedule-jockeying entrant. Under current rules, registering a schedule affords the firm no right other than to operate as registered. A competitor can use schedule jockeying to snatch away the waiting passengers that the incumbent firm's investment has brought to the curb. If the incumbent firm engages in schedule jockeying in response, the tit-for-tat conflict settles into a war of attrition between the two companies. The resulting chaos in service schedules may drive off many riders. The incumbent firm can avoid an ugly war of attrition by simply swamping the route with service. No other reasonable defensive measures are available. Waiting time so dominates passengers' travel decisions that any reputation and amenities an incumbent may offer are not likely to keep waiting travelers from taking the first bus to arrive.[33] Route swamping helps explain why bus-kilometers have increased 17 percent between 1986 and 1991 while total patronage has declined in line with what one would otherwise expect from the fare increase and the long-term decrease in bus ridership.[34]

If one accepts that the ability to swamp a route is necessary to combat schedule jockeying, it is easy to see advantages of larger firms with broader networks. A larger company has more supervisors, drivers, and buses at its disposal that can shift about to swamp a route where a competitor has begun schedule jockeying. A larger company will also have greater financial flexibility to support a route-swamping strategy. Indeed, the very largeness of the firm presents a formidable warning to potential competitors that entry can and will be met by swamping.

32. Dodgson and Katsoulacos (1991, p. 270).
33. Dobson and Nicolaidis (1974); Weismann (1981); Wachs (1992).
34. Gómez-Ibáñez and Meyer (1990, p. 17); Dodgson (1991, p. 123); White (1992, p. 48).

Conclusion

As José Gómez-Ibáñez and John Meyer have commented, "The clearest winners from the combined package of deregulation . . . and subsidy cuts are British taxpayers."[35] Even opponents of deregulation agree that there were considerable benefits to deregulating scheduled bus service in Britain. Most bus companies benefited. The gain or loss to bus riders is hard to determine. Many may have lost from the fare increases or from curtailed service, but many gained from more frequent and more convenient service.

It is not density economies, integration, and so on that lie at the heart of Britain's deregulation experience. The central failing of British bus deregulation is the difficulty that bus companies have had in appropriating their investment in waiting passengers. The result has been schedule jockeying and route swamping, which has disrupted service and diminished competitiveness in the industry. Once again there is a deficiency in the property rights framework leading to a tendency toward monopoly.

With some property rights protection for their investment, incumbent firms would no longer have the need nor the ability to engage in route swamping. Like an inventor enjoying patent protection, they would be able to recoup the value of any investment they make in drawing customers to the curb. Perhaps this incentive would enable the bus industry to reverse the decline of ridership.

The forces that have worked toward greater concentration in the British bus industry would be undermined if not eliminated by a system of property rights. The incentives to absorb small rivals to prevent their interloping would be removed, and companies would no longer need to maintain fighting fleets to use in route swamping. What is more, allowing unscheduled service—jitneys—to pick up passengers at their own curbs would exert market discipline on the incumbent. In essence, unscheduled service enhances both on-the-road competition and contestability.

35. Gómez-Ibáñez and Meyer (1990, p. 18).

Chapter 8

Contracting Out Bus Service in the United States

The escalating costs and the large subsidies required to operate urban mass transit services have led officials to seek private sector participation. In the 1980s the Reagan administration required transit agencies receiving federal subsidies to consider whether the services could be provided by the private sector.[1] Similarly, some small cities and counties that sponsor local transportation services have increasingly relied on the private sector to provide some or all of their fixed-route services, and many transit agencies enlist private firms to operate dial-a-ride and other forms of paratransit.[2] Contracting out allows the public sector to retain planning decisionmaking on routes and fares and types of vehicle to be used, while putting production and operations in the hands of cost-conscious private companies. Contracting out represents a form of privatization, but it is not a form that gives rise to a truly competitive and entrepreneurial market.

Contracting Out: Competition for the Market

Contracting out provides a way to get competition into the provision of services. Although it is only the firm receiving the contract that gets to provide the service, many firms compete to get the contract. In the context of franchise bidding, this is sometimes referred to as competition *for* the market as opposed to competition *in* the market. Competing contenders will offer the best terms they can to

1. Department of Transportation (1984).
2. Teal (1988).

win the contract. The winner is then obliged to live up to the terms of the contract; the law of contract, rather than regulation or internal hierarchy, governs the relationship.[3] Contracting out for bus service is not, strictly speaking, the same as bidding for a franchise contract because much of the compensation comes directly as payment from the agency, but the logic of franchise contracting carries over to contracting out. Contracting therefore may bring competition and entrepreneurship to an otherwise regulated or publicly operated industry. We will revisit the theory of contracting, raising criticisms of this rosy scenario, but first we will review the U. S. experience of contracting out transit services.

Which Transit Agencies Contract Out?

Large transit agencies find it convenient to arrange dial-a-ride services for the elderly and handicapped through contracting with the private sector. Contracting for dial-a-ride services started in the early 1970s when Congress passed a law requiring that no handicapped individual shall be discriminated against in the provision of services that are federally funded. As a result, transit agencies were required to make their buses accessible to the handicapped. Although most agencies equipped their buses with lifts, the inability of handicapped individuals to get to and from bus stops made it difficult to provide services for them using conventional buses. Thus transit authorities implemented dial-a-ride services and contracted some of them with private providers, often with taxicab companies.[4] One-third of dial-a-ride services were contracted out.[5]

Genevieve Giuliano and Roger Teal have identified two forms of institutional structures by which transit agencies are organized.[6] In the *consolidated agency*, funding and operating authority are joined. Regional transit authorities such as the Los Angeles Metropolitan Transit Authority are examples of consolidated agencies. They often have dedicated transit taxes, such as sales or property tax, to operate services. In contrast, the *operating agency* is limited to operating transit services; funding is controlled or allocated by external entities,

3. Demsetz (1968).
4. Gómez-Ibáñez and Meyer (1993, p. 64).
5. Teal (1988, p. 211).
6. Giuliano and Teal (1987).

such as counties, cities, or transportation boards. Consolidated agencies with dedicated funds rarely contract out with the private sector.[7] But when cities without a consolidated agency use general funds to support transit services and have road repair and other municipal services to consider, they tend to find the most effective way to provide transit services. As a result, cities using an operating agency more often contract out some services, bypassing the operating agency, than do their counterparts with consolidated transit agencies.

Similarly, some small transit agencies that have access only to state and local funds are more likely to contract out than comparable transit agencies that have access to federal funds as well. In particular, 49 percent of transit agencies with fifty or fewer vehicles that have access only to state and local subsidies contracted for all their services in 1988.[8] (Even when an agency contracts out bus service, it usually provides and continues to own the vehicles.) But only 23 percent of the transit agencies of similar size that have access to all three sources of funding contracted for all their services. Federal funding carries with it significant restrictions on various aspects of contracted services, including vehicle ownership, Buy America procurement requirements, and other accounting and reporting requirements.[9]

Labor laws are also important in whether a transit agency contracts out. Transit agencies that receive federal subsidies are constrained under section 13(c) of the Urban Mass Transportation Act from taking actions that would harm transit workers. Therefore, if contracting would lead to layoffs of drivers or others or reduce their fringe benefits, transit agencies may not contract out. Moreover, section 13(c) has provided labor unions a powerful bargaining chip to influence policymaking. Thus most transit policymakers are never given decisive authority over whether to contract out.[10]

Results of Contracting Out

Studies have been conducted to determine whether contracting with private providers leads to efficiency gains by reducing costs and subsidies and increasing productivity. In the most widely cited and

7. Teal (1988, p. 215).
8. Teal (1988, p. 215).
9. Cervero (1996, 208ff).
10. Transportation Research Board (1988, pp. 27–32).

extensive research, Roger Teal and colleagues surveyed more than 800 transit agencies throughout the country and found that 35 percent contract for some or all of their services. They found that contracting reduces costs and subsidies by 10 to 50 percent. However, despite the potential savings and the large number of systems that engage in some contracting out, the actual level of service contracted is small, accounting for only 5.1 percent of nationwide transit expenditure, and 8.6 percent of revenue vehicle miles.[11]

In addition to Teal's study, others have examined whether contracting leads to efficiency gains. Some studies have found that there were efficiency gains from contracting, while others found that there were none or there was no difference.[12] The ambiguities stem from the fact that the service bundles provided by the private contractors and the public sector differ. Most private providers, for example, operate only specialized services, such as express commuter services or demand-responsive services. Public agencies provide an array of services. Therefore, because most of the empirical studies did not control for variations in size and scope between the two sectors and other variables, such as the existence of subsidies and labor unions, the conclusions could be biased.

Robert Cervero argues that contracting not only reduces costs on the contracted services, but also provides transit agencies with what he calls "second-order benefits."[13] These benefits emerge as a result of wage and work-rule concessions made by labor unions in an effort to forestall further contracting or to protect their jobs. The concessions often include the elimination of a forty-hour guaranteed work week and allowing the agency to hire part-time drivers. Wayne Talley used regression analysis to determine whether contracting for some services improves the overall cost effectiveness of a transit firm.[14] He found that the Tidewater District Transportation Commission was able to reduce the costs of its regular services by contracting its dial-a-ride services. He maintains that the threat of future cuts in mass transit and Tidewater's plan to convert some of the fixed routes to paratransit services forced the labor unions to make concessions.

11. Teal (1988, pp. 209–12).
12. Perry, Babitsky, and Gregersen (1988).
13. Cervero (1988).
14. Talley (1991).

Two Critiques of Contracting Out

Contracting out is often an improvement over production within a public transit agency. But it is still open to two sorts of criticisms: first, it may be difficult to keep the contracting process competitive; and second, contracting may retain centralized control and choke off entrepreneurial discovery.

The Williamson-Goldberg Critique of Competitive Bidding

Oliver Williamson contends that although contracts might initially be bid on by many competing firms, this does not necessarily imply that a situation in which large numbers of potential contractors are bidding will prevail thereafter.[15] When relationship-specific investments in human and physical assets are needed to support the transaction in question, "contractual asymmetry" between the initial winning bidder and nonwinners will emerge during the contract renewal stage. The initial contract winner learns the job by doing it, giving that one an advantage over other contenders.

A working relationship between a transit agency and a contracted firm requires that the two parties depend on each other for many specific needs. Relationship-specific investments made by one side may give incentives to the other party to behave opportunistically or to hold up operations by demanding new and more favorable terms.[16] As such, the contracting parties will need safeguard mechanisms in their contracts that spell out contingencies and appropriate adaptations. In a world where contingencies cannot be fully delineated, however, the contract must be complex and incomplete. In particular, according to Victor Goldberg, "as the relational aspects of the contract become more significant, emphasis will shift from a detailed specification of the terms of the agreement to a more general statement of the process of adjusting the terms of the agreement over time."[17] Therefore, complex, long-term contracts call for an institutional mechanism to monitor and administer the contract, and to resolve disputes among contracting parties. Operations under such contracts come to resemble internal production of the service by the agency itself.

15. Williamson (1985, p. 61).
16. Williamson (1979); Klein, Crawford, and Alchian (1978).
17. Goldberg (1976, p. 428).

In choosing the duration of a contract, the agency faces a trade-off. A short-term contract keeps the contracted firm on its toes from fear of not winning renewal. But it also discourages the firm from making long-term investments to improve service. A long-term contract has the reverse effects: it encourages long-term investment but reduces competitive pressure.

The criticisms of Williamson and Goldberg apply to the current practices of contracting in the transit industry. Teal found that 47 percent of the contracts are awarded through negotiations and renewals that are not competitively bid. Moreover, when an agency develops an ongoing relationship with a contractor, it is more likely to renew the contract than to let the service out for competitive bidding. Thus although contracting may be a step in the right direction, it seems that it does not really guarantee that even the contest *for* the market will be competitive.[18]

The Discovery Critique of Contracting Out

A simple, optimistic view of contracting suggests that competition *for* the market can closely simulate competition *in* the market.[19] Yet, as we argued in chapter 4, entrepreneurial insight based on local knowledge is best developed within the process of entrepreneurial action. Better knowledge depends on the active and ongoing burden of decisionmaking. The optimistic view of contracting posits that constraints, opportunities, and preferences are known in advance and static; thus the preproduction competition for the market will tap all that competition has to offer. Even the critique by Williamson and Goldberg focuses on the incentive to perform according to the contract; uncertainty simply enlarges the scope and severity of opportunism.

The Hayekian critique of contracting is that new opportunity is discovered throughout the process of providing service by the contract holder, the contracting agency, or some other entrepreneur outside the contract relationship but connected to the market. Exclusive contracting cuts off the seizing of newly discovered opportunity and chokes off the discovery in the first instance.

Both the Hayekian and the Williamson-Goldberg critiques warn

18. Teal (1988, 213ff).
19. Demsetz (1968).

not to expect too much from contracting. The Williamson-Goldberg critique suggests that contracting may not be significantly different from production within the agency. The Hayekian critique suggests that contracting is not likely to measure up to what is achieved in orderly markets with active, ongoing competition. The Hayekian critique suggests that it would be better to devise an appropriate system of property rights to make possible active competition in the market.

Section Three

Property Rights and Route-Based Transit Markets

T he previous section explored a wide variety of transit experiences. Tendencies toward monopolization or collusion in transit services were found in instances involving public transit, regulated franchised transit companies, jitney associations, and contracted operators. Whether a government grants monopoly privileges to routes or leaves the streets as a sort of commons, the tendency is for monopoly to claim its own territory. This section of the book seeks to organize learning from the experiences into a theory of transit markets. The theoretical insights are then used to craft a new proposal that might be able to preserve active and entrepreneurial competition in transit markets.

Chapter 9

A Property Rights Theory of Transit Markets

H ere we build a theory of transit markets on two core premises: jitneys that freely interlope display strong market advantages over scheduled service, and there are significant route-specific sunk costs in developing scheduled service. The theory then considers market conditions for two main variables: the status of curb rights along the route and the volume of passenger demand on the route. The theory encompasses most of the route-based transit experiences surveyed in the previous chapters.

The Market Advantages of Jitneys

The American experience in 1914–16 and that of transit markets in some less developed countries today suggests that jitneys have market advantages over scheduled bus service for both those responsible for providing transit services and for the services' consumers. Because jitney operators follow a route but not necessarily a schedule, they enjoy efficiencies in being flexible with respect to their own schedules and to changes in weather, congestion, time of day, day of week, and so on. Many of the jitney drivers in America in 1915 were part-timers or between jobs; some were simply people going to or from their regular jobs, or young people who borrowed their parents' cars after school. Jitneys enjoy flexibility in negotiating traffic conditions and can make small deviations from the route. Under a free entry policy for jitneys, one could expect a cascade of irregular, short-term participants.

For their part, passengers waiting for a scheduled bus are generally happy to ride a jitney that charges a comparable fare and goes to

FIGURE 9-1. *Market Comparison of Jitneys and Scheduled Services*

Advantages of jitneys
  To providers
    Flexibility for the driver's personal schedule and lifestyle
    Flexibility for the vehicle in usage and schedule
    Flexibility in choosing which routes to ply
    Flexibility in traveling the route
    Flexibility in negotiating traffic
  To passengers
    Available "now"
    Smaller and faster
    Often more pleasant
    Often safer
    Sometimes makes deviations, door-to-door service

Disadvantages of jitneys
  To providers
    Possibly a higher labor cost ratio
  To passengers
    Sometimes less comfortable
    Sometimes less trustworthy

---

the same destination. The interloping jitney offers several advantages. It is available now, whereas the bus is yet to arrive. It is smaller, faster, probably more pleasant, and may offer deviations from its route, perhaps at an extra charge. The bus is cumbersome and dreary; the jitney is entrepreneurial, more personalized, and even somewhat charming.[1] Still, patrons may prefer to wait for the scheduled bus because it offers more certainty and trustworthiness, and it is perhaps more comfortable than the jitney.[2] Figure 9-1 summarizes the market comparisons of jitneys and scheduled services. In what follows we posit that passengers generally prefer to ride in the interloping jitney that charges the same fare as the scheduled service.

1. Takyi (1990, p. 165) notes, "One feature of the Manila jeepney that has made it world famous is its artistic beauty. Its decoration has developed into a true folk art very comparable to that of baroque art. The basic body color (red, blue, yellow, green, and lilac) is embellished with swirling designs of exuberant hue and configuration."
2. Grava (1980, p. 285).

Appropriability of the Investment in Scheduled Service

If, in the presence of scheduled service, jitneys enjoy inherent market advantages, a fundamental issue affecting the fate of scheduled service is whether they are given free run of the streets. It is the issue of curb rights that determines whether jitneying will flourish. In the experiences of America in 1915, of illegal jitneys in America today, and of jitneying in some of the LDC cities, scheduled services do not enjoy curb rights that are fully established and exclusive, either because jitneying is legally permitted or because it is prohibited but not effectively policed against.

Where interloping is both prohibited and effectively controlled, bus companies will invest in establishing routes and schedules, publicizing the information, and running the service in an incipient market because they will be able to appropriate the value of these efforts at bringing people out to the curb. Although transportation economists have found that there are no economies of scale in merely expanding bus service, they have neglected the issue of the appropriability of the investment in setting up and cultivating a route.[3] We maintain that there are specific investments made in cultivating a route and schedule and that the appropriability of these investments depends on curb rights. We assume that because jitneys enjoy inherent market advantages, if they are free to interlope, they will dissolve any scheduled service. Without the anchor of scheduled service, however, it might be that fewer riders will congregate at the curb and thus fewer jitneys ply the route.

Thick and Thin Transit Markets in the Absence of Curb Rights

Another distinction of fundamental importance is whether ridership on a transit route is potentially heavy enough to sustain the cascade of jitneys in the absence of scheduled service. If the market is potentially thick, a situation may develop in which there is no scheduled service, yet jitneys ply the route spontaneously because they have confidence in finding passengers, and passengers congregate at the curb because they have confidence in finding jitneys plying the

3. On the lack of economies of scale, see Viton (1981); Shipe (1992); Hensher (1988).

route. The emergence of conventions that coordinate vehicle services and congregating passengers is found in America today in the cases of some commuter shuttle vans and carpooling practices.[4]

In an inherently thin market this outcome, even if it were to exist at some point, cannot be sustained: there will not be an adequate number of passengers for jitney service to be frequent, and waiting times for unscheduled jitney service will be too long to induce passengers to congregate. Because the coordination problem of unscheduled service is severe in thin markets, service might disappear altogether.

The Thick Market: The Jitney Cascade Is Sustained

Consider the case of the potentially thick market with no exclusive curb rights and thus no scheduled service. The horizontal axis of figure 9-2 shows the number of jitneys per hour that ply the route. The vertical axis shows the number of passengers who congregate at the curb per hour. The figure contains two curves that represent functions which each maps reflexively into the other's domain. The thick line shows the number of jitneys that would come out to serve the route, given a number of congregating passengers. No jitneys serve when there are no congregating passengers, but as congregation grows, the jitneys begin to offer service. In the figure the jitneying response is shown as linear, but it might also be plausible to have the rate of increase declining because of congestion among jitneys. The thinner curved line shows the number of people who would congregate at the curb, given a number of jitneys serving the route. It also starts at zero, then rises at an increasing rate, but because there are only so many people who have any demand at all for jitney service, the curve eventually flattens out.

The curves show the interdependence of the two sides of the market. If only 60 people congregate each hour over the course of a week, about 6.7 jitneys an hour will respond. The next week, people expect about 6.7 jitneys an hour, and therefore only about 50 people will congregate. The next week, jitney operators expect only 50 people an hour, and the jitney function shows that the jitneys come out in even smaller numbers, and so on. For a point to the lower left of point Y, the system degenerates to no market at all, point Z. At

4. Walder (1985); Cervero (1996, p. 97).

FIGURE 9-2. *Interactions between Congregating Passengers and Cruising Jitneys in a Potentially Thick Market*

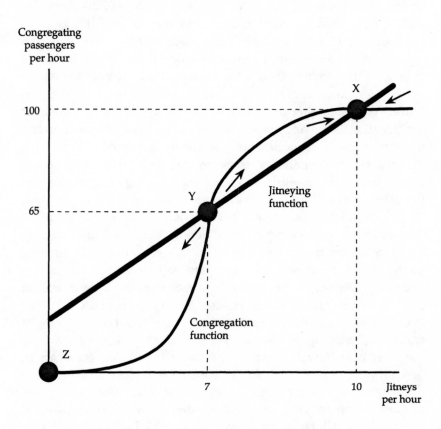

point Z, a stable equilibrium, it would make no sense for any jitneys to ply the route or for anyone to wait for a jitney.

Suppose that a critical mass develops beyond point Y, perhaps due to a transit strike, a coordinated effort by jitney operators, or an unusual event such as the Olympics or a hurricane. In that case the system will maintain life. If, for example, eight jitneys per hour were to ply the route, that would induce significant congregations, which would induce even more jitneys, and the system would bounce up to the other stable equilibrium at point X. Ten jitneys an hour induce exactly 100 congregating passengers, and 100 congregating passengers induce exactly 10 jitneys. This is the realization of potential in a thick market.

The Thin Market: The Dissolving Anchor

Figure 9-3 presents the thin market but also posits that the market begins with scheduled bus service. This is the case of the *dissolving anchor*. The scheduled service begins to operate and builds up a market. At first there is no jitneying, perhaps because jitney operators have not seen an opportunity before the development of this market or because they have not tested the powers of enforcement against interloping. With scheduled service and no jitneys, the number of passengers corresponding to point A waits for the bus. This passenger congregation is the anchor provided by scheduled service. Assume that for some reason jitneying suddenly becomes uninhibited, perhaps because operators come to recognize that enforcement against interloping is weak or nonexistent. They begin to interlope on the scheduled service, and many passengers are willing to take whichever vehicle comes first. The relationship between the upper congregation function (with scheduled service) and the jitneying function implies that the system will be driven to point B, where 9 jitneys ply the route and 100 passengers wait for service. Passengers and jitneys like this outcome, but there is one problem: the scheduled bus is now not getting enough ridership, and it pulls out. The anchor dissolves. Now passengers are less enthusiastic about congregating at curbside. First, they do not have the guarantee of anchor service, so they may have to wait longer or with more uncertainty for a carrier. Second, without scheduled service there is no longer a focal schedule for arrival times at the stops. Jitney arrival times become less predictable. When people go to the curb, they go with less certainty of when a jitney will come, and they wait longer.[5] The decrease in passenger enthusiasm is shown by the shift downward of the congregation function. Nine jitneys an hour now attract fewer passengers. This in turn reduces the number of jitneys, which in turn reduces the number of passengers, and so on. Finally the system settles at point Z, for zilch. Thus the progression is as follows: at point A there is scheduled service; when jitneys interlope, the system moves to point B, the anchor is dissolved, and then the system moves to point Z, or

---

5. It might be thought that once the scheduled service pulls out, the jitneying function would shift outward because jitneys pick up passengers that had been taking the scheduled service. This may not be so because passengers are now more randomly dispersed over the course of the hour due to the loss of schedule focus.

FIGURE 9-3. *Interloping Jitneys Dissolve the Anchor of Scheduled Service and Destroy the Market*

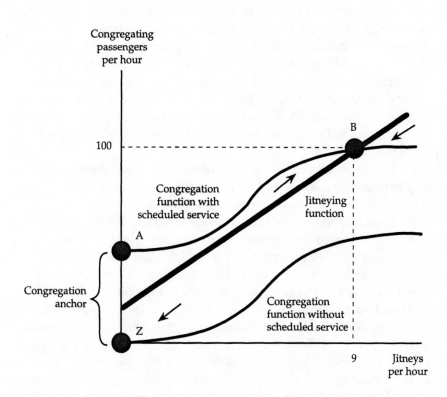

market disintegration. In a thin market the jitney cascade cannot be sustained.

The problem of the dissolving anchor is analogous to the problem of invention in the absence of patent protection. If there is no protection, the inventor sees that he will not be able to appropriate much of the value of his invention because imitations will multiply unimpeded. Therefore the inventor does not invent in the first place. Like inventing, setting up scheduled bus service entails sunk costs: organizing routes and schedules, disseminating information, and running the service at far less than capacity for months until ridership begins to build. Without a system of exclusive curb rights to secure congregations of passengers, interlopers would expropriate the investment. Scheduled service either never begins or does not persist.

A Typology of Route-Based Transit Markets

We suggest a typology of fixed-route urban transit, shown in figure 9-4. The top left cell represents unsubsidized buses with exclusive monopolies on routes with moderate to thin patronage. Exclusive rights are established: there is no interloping and no competition. Therefore scheduled service is preserved. But there are potential problems, the chief of which is inadequate competition and inert monopoly: the incumbent knows that entry is unlikely and consequently skimps on service or increases fares. Another problem is that potential operators will waste resources seeking the rent associated with monopoly privilege.

In the bottom left cell the story is not much different. Again, scheduled service is preserved because interloping is not tolerated. Because the market is thick, it can better support multiple scheduled services, more frequent service, and more consumer choice, but still competition is not tolerated. The problem of inert monopoly is more severe.

The middle cells present cases in which there are no exclusive rights, either because they are not granted or are not enforced. The entire route is essentially a commons. Assuming that there is no impediment to headrunning or interloping, in a thin transit market, shown in the top middle cell, interlopers will headrun on any scheduled service and collect the waiting passengers. This is the dissolving anchor. The lack of property rights in the waiting passengers results in the "tragedy of the commons."[6] The entire market may be destroyed because once the anchor has dissolved, people no longer wait and jitneys no longer ply the route.

The case of the thick market is shown in the bottom middle cell. In this case the lack of curb rights may not be a serious problem. Indeed, any scheduled service will be dissolved, but in a thick market scheduled service may not function as an anchor. Combining elements of figures 9-2 and 9-3, visualize the lower congregation function (without scheduled service) in figure 9-3 as intersecting the jitneying function as does the congregation function in figure 9-2. The market is thick enough to sustain the cascade of jitneys, and riders will be satisfied by flexible, low-cost, and frequent service. This outcome was sometimes found in the American jitney experience of 1915 and exists in a few markets in America today (both illegal and legal) and many of the LDC

6. Hardin (1968).

FIGURE 9-4. *Typology of Fixed-Route Urban Transit*

	Exclusive route for the scheduled service provider	No exclusive rights for scheduled service	No exclusive rights, and scheduled service is subsidized (and charges low fares)
Thin market	Scheduled service preserved Possible problems: inadequate competition and inert monopoly	Interlopers dissolve any anchor Possible problems: market destroyed	Scheduled service monopolizes market Possible problems: subsidy payers unhappy, limited discovery, limited flexibility, inefficiency, politicization
Thick market (potentially)	Scheduled service preserved Possible problems: inadequate competition and inert monopoly	Interlopers dissolve any scheduled service, but a cascade of jitneys offers low-cost, unscheduled service Possible problems: low quality, irregularity, unreliability, untrustworthiness	Scheduled service serves the market, but jitneys may serve excess demand Possible problems: franchising conflicts, subsidy conflicts

transit markets. In any country, however, there are possible problems with the jitney cascade outcome, such as low-quality, irregular service, high uncertainty over terms, and lack of trust. These problems arose with the shuttle vans serving the airport in Los Angeles (see chapter 6).

A case that does not fit into the typology, that would go between the first and second columns, can be imagined. In the British deregulation experience, bus operators enjoy neither exclusive monopolies (column one) nor operate on a pure commons (column two). Rather, free competition is permitted among providers who register schedules in advance. The situation is not that of the pure commons, since freewheeling is not permitted. The British example suggests that nuanced approaches can be fashioned to go between the two extremes of exclusive monopoly and pure commons. We will pursue this idea and propose a property rights framework that avoids monopoly by refining rights along a route.

The cases considered so far have assumed that any scheduled provider could enter the market and that those that do receive no subsidies. We now consider the case in which scheduled service does receive subsidies (notably government subsidies, but much of the reasoning will work also for cross-subsidies). The existence of subsidies usually leads to very low fares. When subsidized service is combined with exclusive curb rights, we get cases similar to those in the first column of figure 9-4. The scheduled service, because it charges low fares, is now even more immune to interloping, so the anchor again is preserved. The likely problems are inadequate competition and the familiar problems attendant on government subsidization.

The results of subsidized, low-fare service without exclusive curb rights are shown in the third column of figure 9-4. Interlopers are free to headrun on the scheduled service, but in this case it is to no avail because patrons decide they will continue to wait for the scheduled bus, which offers a lower fare. Legal jitney services in Los Angeles and San Diego were unable to survive in competition with subsidized public bus fares in the late 1980s (see chapter 5).

The low fares that accompany subsidization provide a new defense against interloping and dissipation of the market. Thus one might defend subsidizing transit on the grounds that curb rights are too costly to establish and enforce, and therefore transit subsidies (and low fares) are the only way to keep scheduled service from being dissolved by interlopers. Subsidization would be a second-best solution where curb rights are too costly to establish. In a thin market, transit subsidization may be the only means to have any transit service at all, even though demand would support transit if that demand were able to express itself in a well-functioning market.

In a thick market, shown in the bottom right cell, the low fares of the scheduled service again will attract riders, but demand might exceed supply. One of the present authors has witnessed transit operations in Shanghai, where low-fare buses are packed sardine-style, and jitneys and taxis cater to the excess demand. In this instance, jitneys survive because of excess demand and because they offer superior quality (less crowding, speedier service), even though they charge higher fares. Further, jitneys charge according to trip distance, so someone traveling a short distance might find the jitney fare competitive with the undifferentiated bus fare.

Although subsidization and low fares may be one way to keep scheduled service from dissolving, we are wary of favoring any kind of subsidization. As spelled out in our discussion of transit fizzle and the public choice critique, subsidization carries problems of its own that outweigh its benefits in preserving scheduled service, regardless of whether the market is thin or thick.

Now, imagine a decision to privatize and deregulate. If public transit and subsidies are eliminated, there remain the first two columns of figure 9-4. These options represent the horns of a dilemma. In one case a provider of scheduled service has a monopoly over the entire route. Because there is no competition, there is little incentive for service improvement and innovation, and fares will be higher. In the other case, no exclusive rights exist. The anchor of scheduled service would be dissolved by jitneys, and markets may never come to be. If policymakers are confined to choosing between these two, they should choose on the basis of whether the market is thin or thick. If the market is thin, they should choose the monopoly because the alternative results in no service at all. If the market is potentially thick, they should choose not to grant exclusive rights to the route and simply allow the jitney cascade to occur. This will bring freewheeling service and competitive energy to the market, whereas the alternative would be inert monopoly.

What would be even better, however, would be an option that avoids either horn of the dilemma, an option that entails a limited degree of exclusive rights to prevent the anchor from dissolving and yet permits freewheeling competition on the route.

Chapter 10

Devising Property Rights for Transit Markets

In the absence of property rights, no one has the incentive to invest because parasites will consume what has been created. Diverse transit experiences have shown rather crude methods of coping with this problem, methods that have tended toward monopolization. In this chapter we develop a more refined proposal for using curb rights and explore the issues raised by the proposal.

Models of Market Parasitism: Interloping, Adverse Selection, and Patent Infringement

Many transit experiences, including those of jitneys in America in 1915, jitneys of LDC cities, contemporary illegal jitneys in New York and Miami, airport shuttles, and deregulated bus service in Britain, show how the entire structure of transit operations often comes down to the crucial issue of curb rights. We have cited reasons to believe that freewheeling jitney operators will always enjoy market advantages over scheduled bus service and will dissolve the anchor of scheduled service if they are free to interlope at bus stops. There is a subtle relationship between the triad of scheduled service, freewheeling jitneys, and the traveling public. To some extent, freewheeling jitneys subsist parasitically on scheduled service, but they do so with the willing cooperation of the traveling public. The parasites in fact place a competitive check on the bus operator's tendency toward inert monopoly. If left unrestrained, however, they might consume the host, and the system dies.

The scenario of the dissolving anchor may be regarded as but one variety of a broader class of models of market parasitism. Another is the insurance model of adverse selection.[1] This model supposes that there are two types of consumers, high risk and low risk, and that only the consumers themselves can know their type. A first company can be actuarially sound by offering a contract that pools both types, and all consumers are better off than they would be with no insurance at all. But the existence of this first company creates an opportunity for a second to enter and offer an insurance contract that the low-risk consumers, but not the high-risk ones, find preferable to the first contract. Thus the low-risk types switch to the second firm. The second firm makes profits when it has only low-risk customers, but the first is left with only high-risk customers. The first firm becomes actuarially unsound and must exit the market. Its departure leaves only one insurance option for the high-risk types: the second company. They enroll with it. Carrying both types, however, makes the second firm unsound, and it must withdraw its contract. In the model there may be no insurance contract that persists as an equilibrium. As with interloping, this is a model of parasitism: the practices of a first company create a profit opportunity for others, but in exploiting that opportunity the others undermine the first and the basis for their own existence.

A similar story of parasitism, parallel to the case of the dissolving anchor, is found in invention and imitation. In performing research and experiments an inventor incurs certain costs. The tangible achievement of his experiments is a new device or process. Similarly, setting up scheduled bus service entails certain fixed costs: planning out routes and schedules, disseminating information, providing benches and shelters, and running the service before ridership has developed, in lean times and in fat. The tangible achievement of these fixed costs is bringing passengers to congregate at designated sidewalk areas. If the provider cannot appropriate his investment, whether in inventing a new device or in creating passenger congregations, because imitators copy the invention or interlopers carry off the patrons, *then he will not invest in the first place*. These incidences of possible parasitism call for a system of property rights.

Consider the two extremes in patent policy. At one extreme is the policy of granting to inventors no patent protection whatever: any

---

1. Rothschild and Stiglitz (1976).

manufacturer is free to use the concept. This policy allows vigorous competition in the manufacturing and marketing of the item once it has been invented, but it reduces the incentive to invent. Now consider the other extreme: every invention enjoys full and exclusive patent protection for all time. This would provide strong incentives to invent, but the inventor of every transistor and ball-point pen would enjoy forever exclusive monopoly control over the concept. If such a policy had always been in place, we would still be paying tribute to the person who invented the wheel. It is obvious that a policy of limited patent protection would be superior to either of the two policy extremes.

Yet in transit policy, cities keep to the two extremes! In the United States, local governments create exclusive monopolies for scheduled bus service by prohibiting competition on the same route. This grants monopoly power and chokes off product differentiation and discovery. It inevitably brings regulation and subsidization, generating a bureaucratic and highly politicized operation. At the other extreme are jitney markets in some LDC cities where there is no curb rights protection and jitneys roam free. This arrangement might be tolerable in thick markets, but in thin markets the jitney cascade will drive out scheduled service, ultimately leaving travelers without any service.

In models of market parasitism, the cooperation of the public is paradoxical in that it is their well-being that competitive enterprise is supposed to serve, but giving them sovereignty to patronize the parasites (whether interlopers, competing insurance firms, or patent infringers) may lead to a condition in which they are worse off. In the case of transit, we propose a new framework that promises to make consumer sovereignty a constructive rather than destructive force in guiding the provision of transit service.

Getting a General Idea of Curb Rights

The framework entails a system of curb rights that both guarantees some exclusivity to those who successfully cultivate passenger congregations *and* gives play to jitneys. Before setting out our thinking about how curb rights might be created, we must emphasize that the spirit of our investigation is exploratory and speculative. If the idea of curb rights is a good one, it must nonetheless be adapted to the particularistic conditions of the public and private resources in which it is being created. A suitable system of curb rights in a given situation will depend on the layout of the streets, the density of travel, the traffic patterns, the availability of vacant curb space and turnouts, the demand for transit, and so on. Not only are the particulars of an individual case multitudinous and complex, but they are different for every case. Furthermore, even if we were to have a good command of the details of a single case, we do not pretend that it would be easy to determine a good system of curb rights. Thus, we know neither the details nor the algorithm. But as Friedrich Hayek would point out, the reasons for the indeterminacy and intellectual intractability of the problem are, indeed, the very reasons for the virtues of a free-enterprise, property rights arrangement. Our understanding of curb rights must itself be a discovery process, built on experimentation, study of results, and evolutionary adaptation and selection of the superior plan by the decentralized and competitive exercise of good judgment. In the following discussion, we do not pretend to offer a tight model: we first introduce basic ideas and then offer refinement and clarification.

The most basic rendition of a curb rights scheme for a thick transit market is shown in figure 10-1. Scheduled bus service has its curb zones, within which it would set up bus stops. When we speak of curb zones or curb rights, it should be understood that we mean not only the curb, but also adjoining space on the sidewalk and road—in other words, a complete bus stop and some additional curb length. These curb zones would be managed by the bus company or some other private party as a private resource. They would be exclusive: jitneys or other buses would be prevented from picking up passengers within these curb zones (unless they received express permission to do so from the holder of the curb right). Scheduled service therefore would be protected from interloping, and the anchor of scheduled service would be preserved.

Along the same route however, jitneys or other services that meet safety and insurance requirements would be permitted to operate. Their pickup places would be at curb areas designated as commons. These areas would have to be laid out around the city in such a fashion as to enable jitney operators to link together some of the commons areas to form a logical jitney route. The commons areas would make possible market entry for all manner of service providers: commuters driving on their way to work who are willing to share the trip, part-time or temporary jitney drivers who work as

FIGURE 10-1. *Example of Exclusive Curbs and Commons*

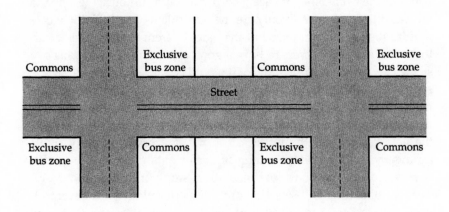

it suits their fancy, independent jitney operators who work on a regular basis, or jitneys organized into associations or company fleets. The scheduled bus that serves the exclusive zones would also be free to stop at the commons. The commons would give life to competition on the route without dissolving the anchor of scheduled service.

Now consider a richer depiction of curb rights arrangements. Consider only one side of the street shown in figure 10-1. That is how to look at figure 10-2, which shows a schematic diagram of curb rights demarcated in both space and time. Consider first just the spatial component, where exclusionary zones are separated by a distance. Think of each exclusionary zone as being 200 feet in length, with the bus stop situated at the midpoint. The column at the 8:00 hour is essentially another version of figure 10-1. It shows that company A is granted two exclusionary curb zones. Yet along the same route, jitneys would operate at the commons.

Temporal Demarcation of Curb Rights

The idea of exclusionary zones may also be defined according to time intervals. Consider now the two peak-period columns, at 8:00 a.m. and 8:15 a.m.. These illustrate the idea that curb zones may be exclusive for company A at fifteen-minute intervals, but then they

FIGURE 10-2. *Property Rights Assignments to Curb Zones*[a]

		8:00 a.m.	8:15 a.m.	3:00 p.m.	3:30 p.m.
	1	A	B	A	B
	2	Commons	Commons	B	B
	3	A	B	A	B
	4	Commons	Commons	B	B

Spatial demarcation of curb rights

Peak   Off-peak

Temporal demarcation of curb rights

a. A denotes a curb right held by company A; B denotes a curb right held by company B.

become the "property" of company B. This system may make enforcement more difficult, but time-elapsed video evidence could show curb rights violations. This principle of exclusionary intervals addresses the central failing of the British experience of bus deregulation: the ability of one company to insert its service just ahead of the competition's. This leads to schedule jockeying and route swamping, which disrupts service and diminishes competitiveness in the industry.

We have argued that in a thin market, giving free play to jitneys could dissipate all service. Off-peak periods often correspond to thin markets. The off-peak times in figure 10-2 show an arrangement that precludes jitneys but accommodates competition on the route by granting exclusionary zones first to company A and then to company

B. Instead of temporal alternation, local authorities might deem it wiser to have spatial alternation of A and B in the same column. Either way, this competitive arrangement would avoid monopoly (unless the two providers were to collude) and would give each provider an incentive to invest in building its ridership. It forgoes, however, the creative and highly efficient input of the freewheelers.

Auctioning Curb Zones and the Emergence of Curb Zone Entrepreneurs

In place of the A's and B's in figure 10-2, envision dollar signs. The authorities could set out exclusive curb zones and simply put them up for sale, perhaps in the form of five-year leases. The leases could be sold at a set price or auctioned off. Auctioning off the curb rights would avoid the hazard of monopoly power that could arise from a maldistribution of initial rights.[2] The holder of curbspace could then run its buses with stops in its leased zones. Under this plan, individuals with local advantages and knowledge of local opportunities could negotiate to make the most of the resource, and the one with the highest valuation would get the curbspace. Further possibilities emerge if the curb rights may be sublet or resold, which we think should be permitted. Company A may then wish to authorize other carriers to pick up in its curbspace and require a monthly rental payment. Or it could resell the lease altogether to a provider with a higher valuation of the curbspace.

We can well imagine the emergence of professional curb zone entrepreneurs who lease available zones from the city, sublet pickup rights to carriers, stage passengers and carriers, and monitor and police the curb rights. These leaseholders could even sublet to jitney associations, but they would manage this competition to protect their interest in their dealings with the scheduled buses. Leaseholders could also profit by using the advertising opportunities on transit benches and shelters.[3] In our visualization of a curb rights system, there would be at least four categories of participants: local officials, curb zone leaseholders, transit operators (bus companies, jitneys, and so forth), and passengers. The rules governing the relations between

2. Hahn (1984).
3. Weisman (1984).

these parties should follow the principles of explicit property rights and contracts, not government ownership or regulation.

Further Issues in Curb Rights

Our sketch of curb rights has so far neglected several important issues. Here we address the issues of enforcement, the emergence of staging areas on private property, the governing of the commons, and the specter of curb zone robber barons.

Enforcement of Curb Rights

Any curb rights scheme will depend crucially on the exclusionary rights of such curbspace being enforceable. Enforceability may not with certainty be feasible, but there seems to be good grounds for optimism. Today in the United States it is only in very exceptional instances, such as in New York City and Miami, that the curb rights of official services are transgressed at all. In Britain where the scheduled service is typically unsubsidized, there is no interloping. Americans are mostly law abiding, and local government can mobilize to protect curb rights.

Harold Demsetz has explained how one's efforts to establish and enforce one's own property rights depend on the costs and benefits of doing so.[4] Thus the local authorities ought to take measures that will reduce the costs and increase the benefits of enforcing curb rights. The holder of the curb rights should be encouraged to monitor the "property." Violations of the rights should be treated as a private tort as well as a municipal violation. Therefore, in addition to municipal enforcement efforts by the traffic or transit police, curb rights holders could do such things as set up enclosed video cameras to watch for repeated trespass. Video footage of trespassing jitneys would simplify identification and apprehension and serve as evidence. Technology and official practice are advancing the photographic enforcement of traffic laws.[5] Furthermore, the drivers of scheduled service could provide eyewitness accounts of headrunning. Suits could also be brought against riders of trespassing

4. Demsetz (1967).
5. Blackburn and Gilbert (1994); Turner (1994).

jitneys. The leaseholder could then put up signs at its bus stops: "Mounting an unauthorized vehicle in this zone is a trespass and subject to civil suit." Travelers would find this reasonable because they could simply walk away from the exclusionary zone to wait legally for a jitney. If there were a sense of curbspace proprietorship and fair competition, both jitney operators and passengers would be likely to respect curb rights.

Emergence of Staging Areas on Private Property

Local officials ought to designate certain curb areas as jitney commons, but they also ought to let additional curb zones or staging areas emerge spontaneously. Officials may wish to manage the emergence of such pickup spots to avoid sidewalk congestion or provide transit focal points, but if certain places seem to be emerging as workable jitney spots, they ought to smile on the development. They may wish to alter parking or standing rules at such spots, and perhaps even provide turnouts, benches, and shelters. Imagine a McDonald's restaurant emerging as a jitneying point, where travelers can buy breakfast and organize shared rides on innovative McTransit.[6] Pickups may take place at the public curb or in McDonald's private lot. If the restaurant began to charge for all-day parking or to cooperate in announcing or arranging jitney departures, this ought to be regarded as legitimate private enterprise. Throughout the city, entrepreneurs may find it profitable to develop jitney staging areas on private property, and jitney associations may want to negotiate a system of such spots with local businesses. In our scheme, local officials are not primarily regulators; they are creators and enforcers of property rights. Provided that jitney operators and staging entrepreneurs do not tread on the property rights of others, they should be allowed to operate unencumbered.

Governing the Commons

An area may be nonexclusive and thus a commons, but nonexclusivity does not mean that anything goes. Even the commons areas will need rules. The commons may be watched over and arranged by

6. Rehmke (1991).

the city, a contracted firm, or a jitney association. Whatever the day-to-day managing agent, local officials should impose guidelines that guarantee open access. A city could offer a windshield certification decal for drivers that meet minimal safety and insurance requirements. Beyond that, there are myriad questions that need consideration. A system of numbered routes, display cards, signposts, electronic boards, or even a curbside coordinator might help coordinate rides. Local officials will need to devise rules or to facilitate agreements among operators on such issues as how long vehicles may wait at the curb and whether they may stop at the commons at all when it is congested.

Curb Zone Robber Barons

Having a market in curb rights might raise the specter of holding companies or robber barons buying up all the curb zones and exercising monopoly power over the route. Local authorities could guard against this in a variety of ways. In a thick market the most powerful discipline is the jitney commons, which allows jitneys to compete with scheduled service. The jitneys represent a direct on-the-road competitor, and the potential of jitney expansion represents the added check of contestability. In a thin market with a monopoly problem, authorities could attempt to see to it that competing providers each have their own curb rights, separated either spatially or temporally. The threat of monopolization at the level of curb rights would also be checked by jitney associations bidding for exclusive rights and developing their own systems of curb zones on private or even public property. In all transit markets, services would have to compete with the automobile and other forms of travel, so even in a market without jitneying, a curb rights monopolist would have to arrange for services that offer terms attractive to the traveling public.

Government Imperfection in Creating Curb Rights

In chapter 4 we invoked public choice analyses to attribute many of the problems with current transit to imperfections in government. We have been proposing, however, a remedy for transit that relies on the exercise of good judgment by local officials in creating curb rights. Are we contradicting ourselves?

To some extent we are, in the sense that our proposed solution would also suffer from government imperfection. We do not pretend that the problems within government somehow vanish when our proposal is pursued. However, virtue is comparative. Any system of transit is bound to rely heavily on government participation because the roadway, the curb, and the sidewalk are government property. Thus any system is bound to be marked by the pitfalls of government imperfection. But in several ways our proposal reduces those pitfalls.

Our earlier analysis of government imperfection was based heavily on the idea that government lacks knowledge of local conditions and therefore is not capable of directing affairs effectively. That problem is reduced when policy is put in the hands of the most local level of government. In our proposal the state and national governments are removed from decisionmaking. We favor a purely local management. Local officials will have much better command of local conditions and local needs. A flexible system of decentralized governance will enable them to use their knowledge and give them cause to dig up more knowledge. In his book on the Bay Area Rapid Transit system, Donald Chisholm contended that a decentralized system of public agencies makes better use of local knowledge than does a unitary public agency.[7]

Another reason that our scheme would mitigate the pitfalls outlined by public choice economists is that it greatly reduces the size and scope of government's involvement in transit. There would be no place for large bureaucracy or large unions. There would be no state or federal money with regulations attached. There would only be officials in charge of devising, enforcing, and refining the property rights framework. The governing of transit by local officials would become disentangled from the many political influences and social goals that now stew in the pot with it. Issues of engine emissions, congestion, and equity would be separated from transit.

In creating a curb rights system, officials in one city may indeed be feckless or corrupt, but the ill consequences would be confined to that city. In our scheme each city would be responsible for its own system of curb rights, and the results would be apparent for the world to compare. Failures in one city would look bad next to the successes of another. Thus there should be some decentralized experimentation to

7. Chisholm (1989).

hit upon good ideas. Then competition and comparison provide a mechanism to encourage the imitation and advancement of good ideas and the reform or abandonment of bad ideas.

Finally, we believe that in our scheme even lackluster governance by local officials would result in a better situation than is usually the case with a municipal transit monopoly under even the most perspicacious management. In our scheme, even if curb rights are ill defined, the door is open to private sector entrepreneurship to make the most of the situation. At the very worst private sector monopolies might develop, but by virtue of cost reductions and innovation, they would be preferable to public sector monopolies.[8] More optimistically, we might expect entrepreneurs to respond by creating their own curbspaces on private property and by forming jitney associations that can bid for exclusive curb rights. The result might be similar to many of the LDC transit systems: jitney associations that operate as cartels. But even this result may be tolerable.

For a variety of reasons, therefore, our proposal, despite its dependence on local officials, is not undercut by arguments of government imperfection because in any alternative institutional arrangement those arguments are likely to bite with at least equal force.

Ideas for Transition Policy

This study is chiefly concerned with delineating a new model for transit policy. It is concerned with drawing a new target for transit policymaking. The question of transition is secondary in our present purpose. We should like to mention, however, that the idea of curb rights does not depend on wiping the slate of transit policy completely clean. Curb rights solutions can be grafted onto existing transit routes, creating either bus stops that compete with current public services or commons areas where jitneys are free to operate. A good transition policy may be to give scope for curb rights developments alongside traditional services and to close down gradually the traditional services as the new, unsubsidized services develop. It may be that cities will find mixed approaches satisfactory, relying partly on free enterprise based on curb rights and partly on franchising routes. Mixed approaches may be especially relevant if there is a po-

---

8. Armstrong, Cowan, and Vickers (1994, p. 111ff).

litical consensus that certain areas need bus service but demand is too low to sustain unsubsidized services.[9]

Conclusion

The unknown possibilities of entrepreneurship would operate to use local knowledge and to discover opportunity. Entrepreneurship works in free markets to produce and sell soap and cornflakes, and it can work for transit once a sensible property rights framework is established. The use of curb rights promises to enable local authorities to achieve the best of both worlds: reliable, scheduled service and real competition, notably from the jitney cascade. Thus many of the problems of transit experiences—lack of on-the-road competition, schedule jockeying, jitney interloping—would be avoided. Because our system defines property rights rather than imposes regulation, it unleashes market forces and minimizes the pitfalls of government control. Curb rights are an antidote to the dismal political cycle of intervention, government takeover, and transit service deterioration.

9. Even if a city were to decide that certain unprofitable bus routes ought to be subsidized, it may be possible to do so within a free-enterprise curb rights arrangement by offering subsidies to patrons or subsidizing producers by awarding them a percentage bounty on fare receipts.

Chapter 11

How Property Rights Resolve Problems of Free-Market Transit

Ａn artless proposal of free competition for route-based transit—unregulated operation of buses and jitneys with no particular system of bus stops or curb rights—should raise serious objections and doubts of the success of such a system. More refined proposals for market-based transit might be less susceptible to criticism, depending on the specifics of the proposals. This chapter examines broad criticisms lodged against market-based transit. The criticisms are that it results in cutthroat competition, fails to achieve economies of density, results in discoordination of transit connections, fails to provide good consumer information, causes curbside conflict, and fails to provide adequate passenger facilities.

In assessing the merit of each criticism, we assume a sophisticated transit context of curb rights based on the ideas presented in chapter 10. Suppose that a large metropolitan area such as Los Angeles has shut down its transit services, sold off its vehicles, and declared a free-competition policy for all bus and jitney services. The only requirements that the local government retains for market entry are a driver's license, vehicle insurance and registration, and safety certification. Entrepreneurs both large and small begin offering their services. We would expect vehicles to be buses, owner-operated vans, and even ordinary sedans, and would also expect the gradual development of brand names and operator associations. Operations take place within a system of curb rights. Local officials define curb zones, auction them off, allow staging areas on private property, and assist in enforcing the corresponding rights. Curb rights holders may sublet their curbspace to other carriers or resell their leases. Jitney commons and competing exclusive curb zones are assumed to be created by local officials as appropriate to market conditions.

When free-market transit takes place within this kind of well-devised framework of curb rights, the various criticisms of it can be answered convincingly—in fact, better answered than by the alternative systems that have governed transit markets.

Cutthroat Competition

Some observers are concerned that free-market transportation will engender cutthroat competition, an idea originally developed in the context of railroads and public utilities.[1] And there is indeed some reason to consider the criticism. Fixed costs for a network of bus service may include costs of planning routes and schedules, disseminating information, and cultivating market demand.[2] If these costs are both high and sunk and marginal cost is low, competition may drive firms to cut prices to such low levels that costs cannot be recouped.

In the criticisms of free-market transit, cutthroat competition may develop in various ways and result in very different outcomes. Suppose company A sets up a bus system. Perhaps there is some call, in a blackboard sense, for a second firm. Company B enters the market, but the tendency toward price cutting is too strong and both firms are ruined. One variation on the story is that company B is smart enough not to enter, in which case company A enjoys an unrestricted monopoly. Because company A can easily and promptly cut prices in the event of entry, there is not much discipline exerted by potential new competitors. Another variation is that company B enters and the two firms, recognizing that there is neither profit nor sport in cutthroat competition, collude or merge. In these situations prices remain well above marginal cost and ridership remains correspondingly low. Indeed, it is often argued that, because the marginal cost of an additional rider is very low, urban transit ought to charge very low prices and receive subsidies.

There are reasons to doubt whether the idea of cutthroat competition characterizes any industry fairly, depending as it does on as-

1. See Keeler (1983), pp. 22, 470; Savage (1985, 1986b).
2. Nash (1988, p. 112).

sumptions that cost conditions are identical for all competitors, all have full knowledge of cost conditions, that they are single-product firms, that service is homogeneous, and so on. But observers have pointed out that cost conditions are not given and argue that the benefit of discovery and innovation from competition may well out-weigh the social costs of duplicating firm-level sunk costs.[3]

Taking the theory on its own terms, however, there are reasons to believe that a curb rights framework would defuse the problem. First, in thick markets jitneys would operate along the same routes as scheduled service. Picking up passengers at designated commons, the jitneys would not face the fixed costs associated with setting up a scheduled service. Thus scheduled service, even if provided by only one bus company, could be expected to retain competitive fares and services. The jitneys would, then, guarantee a competitive fringe—or even a competitive mainstream—in the market. The scheduled service could maintain its presence by virtue of its special service characteristics and its exclusive curb rights.

Even in thin markets, local authorities could prevent consolidation of curb zones (or time windows at the curb). Reselling or subletting curb rights can be restricted to prevent mergers or monopolization. Shopping mall owners make sure that customers have more than one dining service to choose from, and local officials can do likewise for transit services. An antimonopoly policy might be misapplied, pre-venting a more efficient firm from expanding its market, but it would be available to prevent egregious collusion or monopoly power.

Some commentators have likened route swamping in Britain to cutthroat competition as one firm invests heavily in predatory be-havior.[4] The problem in Britain, however, is that after the incumbent has cultivated the market, competitors can register service to match its schedule. The inability to appropriate one's investment in setting up scheduled service has created the situation. A curb rights plan would solve this problem.

The British experience also highlights the importance of contesta-bility. Even where on-the-road competition does not occur, incumbent companies face the threat of entry. Traditional theory suggests that with free entry, a market is more contestable the lower sunk costs are,

3. Hazlett (1985); Armstrong, Cowan, and Vickers (1994, p. 107ff).
4. Nash (1988, p. 112); Dodgson and Katsoulacos (1991); Savage (1993, p. 146).

the longer it takes the incumbent to reduce prices in response to entry, and the more alike the products of the entrant and incumbent.[5] Jitneys offer a service similar to that of scheduled buses and have very low sunk costs. In a potentially thick market, if a bus company raises prices or cuts service, jitneys might rapidly expand to cater to disgruntled customers. Even if the market is unlikely to attract competing scheduled services, the ease of jitney entry and exit by virtue of the existence of commons areas enhances contestability.

Failures to Achieve Economies of Density and Coordination of Transit Pieces

Another criticism of free-market transit is the argument stemming from economies of density. Although bus service does not show economies of scale in production, there are systemwide gains from increased volume.[6] Part of the gains may come in the form of lower production costs due to larger vehicles. But gains also accrue to riders from the shorter waiting times associated with more frequent service and the shorter walks to pickup points that are associated with denser route structures.[7] These gains for consumers can be interpreted as improvements in service quality, which in turn will increase demand for service.

Christopher Nash has contended that the free-market process of "piecemeal infilling of gaps" will not successfully achieve economies of density.[8] Operators of individual transit services will not take into account the systemwide benefits flowing from their actions to increase the volume of patronage. They neglect to consider the potential systemwide patrons that their operation cannot capture and other benefits that accrue in other pieces of the system. Because of these impediments to achieving economies of density, free-market incentives will not function properly.

A related criticism maintains that piecemeal operators will inevitably fail to coordinate schedules to achieve smooth through-ticketing and connections among individual transit pieces. Riders will be frus-

5. Baumol, Panzar, and Willig (1982); Morris and others (1986); Armstrong, Cowan, and Vickers (1994).

6. Viton (1981); Hensher (1988); Shipe (1992).

7. Mohring (1972); Gwilliam, Nash, and Mackie (1985a, b).

8. Nash (1988, p. 118).

trated in trying to connect the various legs of their journeys and will have to make a separate transaction for each. Nash has asserted that again there are systemwide benefits from through-ticketing and schedule coordination, benefits that individual operators would ignore. He combines this coordination argument and the density argument to make a case for transit integration, or central planning.

Even if piecemeal operators were to coordinate schedules and permit through-ticketing, a decentralized transit system might suffer because consumers are given inadequate information. Passengers might be unsure of fares or routes and cause delays by inquiring of drivers, asking for change, making payments, and so on. They might have an especially hard time in learning the routes and fares of independent jitneys.

Density effects and disjointed pieces are certainly common, and in that sense these criticisms have an obvious validity. But the very pervasiveness of the problems leads one to doubt that they make transit a significant departure from normal market conditions. One of the reasons private organizations often grow to enormous size is to coordinate diverse activities centrally or to achieve economies of scale and scope, which are akin to economies of density.[9]

Density economies can be considered similar to the advantages of the division of labor discussed by Adam Smith. A thicker transit market allows larger vehicles, a denser route structure, shorter walks to the bus, and shorter waiting times. But such benefits also ensue from using private automobiles. If people drive cars rather than take transit and the government builds more roads instead of subsidizing transit, the markets for auto sales, parts, repairs, and fuel will expand and the road system will be more efficient. As another example, consider a person who decides to become a saxophone instructor in an area that already has some instructors. Saxophone students will have shorter distances to travel, greater flexibility in arranging lessons, and some product differentiation. It may be true that density effects are especially important in transit services, but how much more important than in other services? Economies of density are notoriously hard to measure.[10] Transit may not in fact display them significantly more than do other typical uses of taxpayer money.

9. Coase (1937); Chandler (1990).
10. Caves and others (1985).

Even if density economies were peculiar to transit, there would remain the question of whether a centralized government authority would realize them better than free enterprise would. Appropriate integration to realize the economies and create smooth interchanges would depend on knowing where such benefits lay and what forms they take. One might break up the question into two parts: what are the market conditions and opportunities and what are the incentives for providers to make welfare-enhancing actions in service. When Nash compared central planning with the free market, he assumed that in either regime providers are *omniscient* about market conditions. Thus he swept aside the chief question: how do providers (and potential providers) gain and use knowledge. Sweeping this question aside biases the comparison because one virtue of free enterprise is its ability to dig up new and better knowledge. It is no wonder that analysts who assume the ready availability of all relevant knowledge tend to discount the free enterprise system. As Friedrich Hayek remarked, "If anyone really knew all about what economic theory calls the *data*, competition would indeed be a very wasteful method of securing adjustment to these facts."[11]

In real life one has to compare the imperfect knowledge of one system with that of the other. Service planned by public officials is not especially effective in discovering new knowledge. Inefficient systems often persist due to bureaucratic inertia and procedural and cognitive lock-in. Gabriel Roth and Anthony Shephard have reported that one city transport manager in Britain estimated it takes up to eighteen months for a franchised operator to make a schedule change.[12] Furthermore, the idea of integrated planning is somewhat illusory. Executives of large public agencies may not really command the knowledge that resides in the diverse offices and departments of the agency.[13] One department may make mistakes because it does not know things that are commonplace to employees in another. There is no reason to assume that knowledge is integrated just because all of an agency's employees work in the same building.

As for the incentive to make welfare-enhancing changes in services, Nash again accords government officials the status of superior

11. Hayek (1978, p. 179).
12. Roth and Shephard (1984, p. 70).
13. Chisholm (1989).

beings. They are assumed to want nothing but to maximize social welfare. Thus he neglects all the public choice learning about how real-life public officials behave, notably in large public agencies.

Private entrepreneurs in Nash's model are assumed to be self-limiting in their scope of action. Because density and interchange benefits extend beyond these separate operators, private entrepreneurs, he contends, develop service at levels that are less than optimal. But one ought to question whether free-enterprise transit is bound to operate in such a piecemeal fashion. It might be said that entrepreneurs are in the coordination business; they are deal makers. Wherever private taxis, jitneys, or buses have provided services, organizations of firms or associations of operators have almost universally followed. Route associations, company fleets, organization representatives, and agents all function to take into view the connections and network effects. The creation of curb rights, furthermore, would introduce holders of the rights, who are specifically interested in the connection between different bus or jitney lines. The holders would have an obvious incentive to coordinate schedules and encourage smooth interchange because market demand for services intersecting at a given curb (or network of curbs) would directly affect the value of a holder's rights. Bus companies will have an especially strong incentive to take advantage of interchange benefits if there is head-to-head competition on their route, which is likely in our curb rights scenario. Offering patrons smooth and convenient connecting services would be one way to outdo the competition.

We can well imagine industry associations of carriers or curb rights holders that discuss and plan timetables and through-ticketing arrangements. With electronic debit cards and other new technologies, through-ticketing in any transit system is much less difficult to set up than it once was. And just as newspapers publish movie timetables, interested parties could communicate with patrons by disseminating timetables and information about through-ticketing and fares. Carriers or curb entrepreneurs might organize to establish a telephone service that tells callers how to piece together their trips. Curb rights holders would have a strong incentive to publicize the information with signs, printed schedules, and so on.

As for traffic management at the jitney commons, a simple system of signs could be established for patrons and drivers. A number on a sign could refer to the destination or route and a color could represent fare scales or service options. Different places at the curb could serve as staging zones for different routes. Local jitney registration and safety certification could be displayed on the exterior of the vehicle's passenger-side door. Perhaps a curbside coordinator could be designated for each jitney commons to assist staging.

Even in the implausible case in which the individual operators did not look more than one link beyond their bailiwick, they would be alert to an opportunity to coordinate with that next link. In so doing, a nexus of voluntary planning would emerge among transit providers. In his book on economic planning, Don Lavoie offers an analogy: "Termite colonies have the remarkable ability to regulate precisely the temperature of their intricately constructed and often gigantic hills by sophisticated ventilation techniques that would surely perplex the cleverest single termite."[14] Piecemeal operators, like myopic termites, might not see the big picture, but they might be able to recognize an opportunity for increased patronage and smooth connections and be quick to seize it. The aggregate effect of such local activities might be a complex and fluid system, one that emerges more by accretion and serendipity than by design.[15]

Curbside Conflict and Inadequate Passenger Facilities

Critics of freewheeling jitneys sometimes raise the problems of dangerous driving and curbside conflict as reasons for strong government control. One can imagine competing van drivers battling for customers on the busy main routes.[16] Fistfights at the curb or accidents involving pedestrians could ensue.

Another matter is providing the benches, shelters, stations, signs, and other passenger facilities that are important complements to transit services. Indeed, if carriers operate under laissez-faire, local authorities might have difficulty coordinating the provision of these facilities. The operators might lack an impartial representative to work with the local authorities, and the market might itself be in constant flux. Waiting passengers might begin to accumulate at places where they impede pedestrian traffic or access to businesses.

But it is important to remember that public transit uses public

14. Lavoie (1985, p. 27).
15. Alchian (1950).
16. Grava (1980).

commons: the roadway, the sidewalks, and the bus stops. Public bus stops are often unsafe and ill maintained. A curb rights regime would create private holders of curbside facilities. They would have the incentive and much independent authority to provide the appropriate facilities and to police them to ensure good conduct and trustworthiness. Not only could great improvements in safety and comfort be expected, but also improvements in security. Such actions would be simply part of serving the customer.

Conclusion

The various doubts about the feasibility of free-enterprise transit—about the emergence of cutthroat competition, impediments to economies of density, poor system coordination, inadequate information for patrons, and difficulties with curbside facilities—all depend on the nature of the property rights framework within which free enterprise functions. As Hayek commented, "the functioning of a competition . . . depends, above all, on . . . a legal system designed both to preserve competition and to make it operate as beneficially as possible."[17] The curb rights system should largely dispel the traditional criticisms of free-enterprise transit.

17. Hayek (1944, p. 38).

Section Four

Policy Recommendations and Conclusions

O ur survey began by noting the triumph of the automobile and presented the primary reasons—based on Hayekian and public choice analysis—for the failure of traditional transit. We have explored various transit experiences and features of free-market transit, both its virtues and vices. We have also presented the salient fundamentals of transit issues.

We proposed in chapter 10 a property rights framework for route-based transit designed to give full vigor to private entrepreneurship. The proposal forms the core of our policy recommendations, but we will not repeat it here. Instead, we turn to a brief discussion of further policy recommendations. These recommendations are not required for a property rights approach to function, but they would improve its effectiveness. We also address issues aside from route-based transit, notably taxi markets.

Chapter 12

Further Policy Recommendations

The serious, even drastic, policy reforms we are about to propose reflect our sense of the fundamentals of urban transit. The proposals overlap somewhat, but we treat each of them as if it stood alone, though there may be increasing returns to adopting all of them. We restrict ourselves to an overview of the proposals and do not address the immediate issues of policy feasibility and gradual transition. This is not to suggest that the immediate issues do not call for attention. If there is to be any real hope of reform, they must be attended to in detail. But our purpose is to set out, for the consideration of policymakers, long-term destinations for policy reform. Think of these proposals as establishing a context within which our main proposal of transit systems based on curb rights can fulfill its potential. We hope that our proposals will aid policymakers in forming a better idea of what they should be working toward. Some might disparage our approach as impractical or utopian, but paying attention to fundamentals is the only way to gain farsighted vision as well as insights for the here and now.

1. Deregulate All Transit Services

Because much transit regulation is based on faulty justifications and produces perverse results, the law must clearly limit the aspects of transit services that authorities are permitted to regulate. Authorities should be able to require only that a transit service provider have a valid driver's license, vehicle registration, and insurance and that its vehicles undergo periodic safety inspections. This restriction should apply to all levels of jurisdictional authority and to all forms of transit service: buses, jitneys, shuttles, shared-ride taxis, taxicabs, and so on. Given a property rights framework, one can expect transit services to develop trademarks, brand names, and association identifiers. These are the normal market institutions that sustain quality and trustworthiness.[1] Their presence would diminish the need for safety regulation.

2. Dissolve Public Transit Agencies and Sell Off All Public Transit Capital

It makes no more sense for government to produce transit than it does for government to produce cornflakes. The basic Hayekian and public choice teachings apply here in full force, and every bit of more specific learning shows that government is characteristically inept in providing transit. Virtually all public transit agencies should be drastically reduced and redirected, and all public transit vehicles and other plant and equipment should be sold off. Of course lobbying and political influence will intrude into and affect any process of privatization.[2] But there are many successful methods of auctioning off public sector resources.[3] The British experience provides an example of privatization that worked reasonably well.

3. End Federal Involvement

Privatizing transit services would eliminate the justifications often proffered in support of subsidies. Federal involvement in local transit comes mainly through Federal Transit Administration capital and operating subsidies. The program came into being in response to blatant rent seeking by large cities, and the subsidies amount to redistributing wealth from rural or suburban dwellers to transit systems that serve the central city. Because local transit agencies would be limited to managing curb rights and possibly a few other responsibilities discussed in this chapter, there would be no need for further subsidies. All of this is true also of state subsidies, and they should eliminated as well.

1. Klein (forthcoming).
2. Vickers and Yarrow (1991).
3. Savas (1982); Poole and Fixler (1987); World Bank (1988); Graham and Prosser (1991).

Taxpayers would not be the only beneficiaries. In the absence of subsidies, local transit decisions would no longer be so distorted. Forced to pay for themselves, grandiose schemes and wasteful monuments such as Los Angeles's Gateway Intermodal Transportation Center would no longer entice local authorities.[4] These officials would also no longer be tempted to pursue urban renewal or job growth with transit project funds.[5] Mobility needs rather than politics would again be the driving force behind decisions affecting transit.

The elimination of subsidies would actually have advantages in meeting mobility needs. State and federal subsidies bring with them restrictions on local employment, purchasing, and service decisions. For example, section 13(c) of the Urban Mass Transportation Act restricts local authorities from using federal subsidies in ways that might require layoffs or wage reductions for transit union employees. Local financing would return the focus of transit decisions to local needs and opportunities.

4. Create a Nested Commerce Clause for Jurisdictional Authority

There will always be a temptation for local interests to lobby for special privileges. Likewise, some public officials will always find an excuse to intervene in transit decisions. In our plan, clear and simple constraints describing the limits of authority would be placed on each jurisdictional level. Such an approach must specify which level of jurisdiction has regulatory authority for each transit service. We propose a nested jurisdictional authority clause in the spirit of the interstate commerce clause of the U.S. Constitution.

Any transit service that crosses a jurisdictional boundary should

---

4. The Transportation Center is a project costing $325 million to provide a joint rail and bus station on the edge of downtown Los Angeles. It includes a new twenty-six-story office building, of which the Metropolitan Transit Authority would occupy only a few floors. Meanwhile, throughout the downtown the rental rates for office space are well below building costs and there is a 24 percent vacancy rate (Ferguson 1995).

5. The idea that greater transportation infrastructure increases productivity, which might have positive effects on the whole region, has been fairly well discredited. See Giuliano (1989); Boarnet (1994); Gramlich (1994); Holtz-Eakin (1994); Kelejian and Robinson (1994). Some of these studies show that new roads do not usually stimulate a net increase in productive activity; they merely shift traffic from areas less well served by roads.

be regulated only by the encompassing level of authority. For example, a jitney service that operates on a route running through two cities could not be regulated by the cities, but only by county or regional authority. Likewise, a taxi service that operates across a county line could not be regulated by a county, but only by regional or state authority. This will prevent local protectionism and perhaps help ameliorate disjointed service. Curb rights, however, would remain the responsibility solely of the immediate local government.

5. Create Locally a System of Curb Rights for All Route-Based Transit

An exposition of curb rights, the core of our proposal for route-based transit, is developed in chapter 10. Here we wish only to discuss the local nature of this proposal and the many peculiarities to be dealt with.

Because the conditions of time and place are particularistic and always changing, successful entrepreneurship and effective exploitation of markets depend on local knowledge. In proposing a strongly localized approach to urban transit, we extend the emphasis on local knowledge to the devising of property rights by public officials. Hoping that officials will pursue what we believe will work best for transit, we urge them to study local conditions in crafting the property rights that underlie transit markets.

There are no fail-safe principles, but intelligence, experience, and comparative study can help answer many relevant questions. How many years should curb rights leases last? How many yards long should the exclusionary zone be? How many minutes apart should the exclusive time windows at curbside be? How many commons curbs for jitneys should there be? Should local authorities provide turnouts? Should they provide benches and shelters or leave that to the lease-holders? How should they cope with congestion at the curb? Should carriers be restricted from dropping off passengers in exclusive curb zones? These and other questions are local matters to be investigated and decided by local officials, the way that officers of a proprietary community decide contracts and resource use. Chapter 10 provides the fundamental idea: break down curbspace into numerous pickup zones, some exclusive and transferable and some nonexclusive, and allow entrepreneurship to build services from these cornerstones.

Besides the curb rights issues, many of our ideas—selling off all transit capital, requiring safety inspections, providing passenger subsidies, setting up a taxi watchdog agency—also depend on local conditions and the judgment of local officials. Although public choice analysis suggests that public officials often lack strong incentives for good performance, our plan would to some extent depend on the intelligent decisionmaking of local officials. We believe, however, that compared with the paradigm of regulation and government ownership, the property rights approach depends less on the good faith, imagination, and hard work of people in government and more on private sector entrepreneurs with normal qualities and motives.

6. Institute Highway Pricing

Although many lament the triumph of the automobile, we regard the automobile as an unambiguous vehicle of betterment. It is both cause and consequence of widespread prosperity. Nonetheless, it ought not to be indiscriminately favored. It too should pay its own way, and in a sensible manner. The best means available is highway pricing: toll revenues should pay for highways, and drivers should be charged for causing highway congestion. In making the private auto pay its own way, transit would be made more competitive. Commuters traveling in shared-ride vehicles would pay only a fraction of the toll. High-occupancy vehicles may even travel free, as they do on the new median lanes toll road of state route 91 in Orange County, California.[6] This would give commuters new incentives to travel by carpool, subscription van, or commuter bus. Road pricing is good highway policy and good transit policy.

7. Consider Rider Subsidies to Meet Equity Goals

Government involvement in urban transit, through subsidies or public provision, creates inefficiencies and invites political intervention. Nonetheless, some communities may wish to ensure transit services for persons who are not otherwise well served by private providers. If, based on equity or other reasons, a community wishes to subsidize transit use, we recommend that they do so only at the local level, where administrators' experience and local knowledge

6. Fielding and Klein (1993).

can be used to best advantage. Staying local also reduces the number of interest groups tempted to get involved, narrowing the scope of rent-seeking problems. We recommend passenger subsidies be used. By providing vouchers directly to the persons to be subsidized, the community allows the market to determine the best way to provide the service. Apart from paying for the subsidy, a transit voucher plan conforms nicely to the property rights approach to transit. Transit entrepreneurs are still private, and they still compete by offering their services to paying customers.[7]

8. Reform Taxi Policies to Cope with Consumer Information Problems

Chapter 11 discussed the inadequacies of consumer information on route-based services. Here we focus on problems of consumer information about edge transit services, especially taxis that are hailed or selected from a queue. The telephone market for cabs is much less problematic because callers can easily inquire about fares and ponder the alternatives.

With taxicabs in a queue at an airport and a stand operator instructing passengers to take the lead cab, there is no means of introducing competition based on price or quality, and unrestricted fares could mean severe price gouging. When taxis are free to roam at an airport and cabbies enter the terminal to solicit passengers, visitors experience a general sense of chaos. Even researchers such as Sandra Rosenbloom and Bill Styring who are sympathetic to taxi deregulation maintain that fare deregulation in an airport market might create severe problems.[8] Most cities have reinstituted price ceilings on taxi service originating at airports.[9]

There are two general solutions for problems in the airport taxi market: either the airport should manage service and fare differentiation with multiple taxi stands and a designated coordinator to aid passengers, or uniform rates should be set for all trips originating at the airport. Because many travelers emerge from a terminal in a state of bewilderment and terminal traffic is heavily congested, fare regu-

7. Kirby (1982) reviewed a number of these transit subsidy programs and reported good results. See also Cervero (1996, p. 49).

8. Rosenbloom (1986, pp. 15, 18); La Croix, Mak, and Miklius (1985); Kirby's comments following LaGasse (1986); Styring (1994, p. 35).

9. Cervero (1996, p. 49).

lation often will make the most sense. But municipal authorities ought to devolve the regulatory decisionmaking to airport authorities, who know more about local resources, have more incentive to serve travelers, and have less motive to confer monopoly rents on service providers. Airport practices could emulate those at hotels, where doormen shepherd patrons to the appropriate transit services and exclude problem operators.[10]

Information about fares in all taxi markets might be improved by requiring a uniform measure. For instance, if a taxi establishes rates by distance, it must set its flag drop charge for the first one-fifth mile and charge for every one-third mile of additional travel.[11] Imposing such units for rates would facilitate fare comparisons. Taxis could set the flag drop charge high enough to make short trips worth their while. They also ought to be permitted to use other rate structures— zones, journey duration, time of day, and so forth—but be required to use a uniform measure of distance if they elect to charge by distance.

Another way of alleviating consumers' lack of information is for an organization to perform watchdog services regarding taxi trustworthiness and gather information in the way that *Consumer Reports* does to help consumers comparison shop. The organization's members could gather information on the fares and service quality of the various fleets or associations and go undercover as customers to check on trustworthiness. The resulting information could be distributed to airports, travel agents, hotels, tourist centers, information booths, apartment buildings, hospitals, and senior citizen communities. It could also be printed periodically in local newspapers.

Private organizations akin to Underwriters' Laboratories, Better Business Bureaus, or Consumers' Union would make the best providers of these services. They might charge for the information or might be funded by local civic organizations. Bus operators and curb entrepreneurs might form an association to have the quality of their own services policed in this manner. If the market response is not sufficient, local government may wish to contract the job to a private firm. We do not urge government to get involved in consumer reporting for route-based services because curb rights holders would have a direct interest in doing so.

10. See Reinke's comment following Rosenbloom (1986, p. 18)*
11. Doxsey (1986, p. 8).

Chapter 13

Conclusion: Transcending the Choice between Monopoly and Lawless Competition

A round the world a broad-based change in attitudes is in progress, a movement away from dependence on government regulation and government ownership and toward a new emphasis on property rights and private sector enterprise. For generations the mixed-economy thinking of American public transit policymakers has led to extensive regulation and government intervention. We believe that the property rights system needs to become the core of transit policy, and this study has described how this change can be accomplished.

To this end we have delineated a number of transit markets. First, there are commuter services, door-to-door shuttles, and taxis. Not only do we regard current regulation of these services as patently unjustified, but instituting a system based on private enterprise and property rights for them would be straightforward: allow free entry into the market and free enterprise, with minimal insurance and safety requirements. In the case of trips originating at airports, there may need to be some additional oversight to avoid confusion and unduly high fares. But the context of a property rights system suggests that airport authorities, who would be regarded as independent property holders, can set the necessary additional rules and guidelines. They can arrange with taxis to charge a uniform price, wait in appropriate holding areas, and accept passengers in an orderly fashion. Citywide regulation is unnecessary.

The most difficult, most important, and most interesting challenge is to remake route-based service. Despite federal, state, and local subsidies to municipally owned bus services, ridership in this country has been dwindling for many years and productivity has declined. But route-based service can be reinvigorated. We have developed a theory of scheduled service that recognizes the importance of generating passenger congregations, that is, sufficient riders at scheduled stops to form a kind of critical mass of ridership. But to succeed, a transit operator's investment in cultivating passenger congregation through dependable service, attractive vehicles, advertising, and so forth must be recoverable, which means the service must be protected from interloping by jitneys (route-based but unscheduled vehicles), gypsy cabs, and the like.

Many studies of markets here and abroad show that transit operations are gored by one of the two horns of a transit dilemma. Some markets enable scheduled operators to appropriate the value of passenger congregations, but this is achieved by granting them exclusive rights, not only to the passengers waiting at specific curb zones but to the entire route itself. Thus the first horn is transit monopoly. Other markets, especially those in some less developed countries, avoid all regulation, which not only precludes transit monopoly but indeed gives rise to freewheeling competition. It also impales transit service on the other horn of the dilemma. Scheduled service does not cultivate passenger congregations because constant interloping will expropriate the investment. In consequence, densely populated, thick markets are somewhat chaotic with unpredictable service and thin markets lack the anchor needed to sustain any service at all.

A carefully planned transit system based on property rights can, however, avoid either horn of this dilemma. American cities can have the best of both kinds of markets, scheduled (and unsubsidized) bus service and unscheduled but faster and more flexible jitneys. Figure 13-1 revises figure 9-4 by inserting our solution between exclusive monopoly and the unregulated commons.

The solution is based on a new idea, a previously unnoticed policy opportunity: create exclusive and transferable curb rights (to bus stops and other pickup points) leased by auction.[1] This way sched-

---

1. There appear to be parallels to our curb rights approach in other services. For natural gas, rail, and electricity service, the service provider and the customer must link up on a network that neither owns. The difficulty is to make the connections possible without encouraging interloping and without imposing a monopoly. Works that explore property rights solutions in these services include Starkie (1993) on rail, and Smith, DeVany, and Michaels (1990) on natural gas.

FIGURE 13-1. *Typology of Unsubsidized Fixed-Route Urban Transit Incorporating the Property Rights Solution*

	Exclusive route for scheduled service	Refined system of curb rights for scheduled service	No exclusive rights for scheduled service
Thin market	Scheduled service preserved Possible problems: inadequate competition and inert monopoly	Scheduled service preserved Potential for competing scheduled services; commons provides jitneying opportunities	Interlopers dissolve any anchor Possible problems: market destroyed
Thick market (potentially)	Scheduled service preserved Possible problems: inadequate competition and inert monopoly	Scheduled service preserved and jitneys offer low-cost, unscheduled service	Interlopers dissolve scheduled service, but jitneys offer low-cost, unscheduled service Possible problems: low quality, irregularity, untrustworthiness

uled service would have exclusive protection where its passengers congregate, and jitneys would be able to pick up passengers elsewhere along the route, at curb zones designated as commons. Our plan would thus rid the transit market of inefficient and expensive government production and overregulation. It would also avoid the potential imperfections of a lawless market: cutthroat competition, schedule jockeying, a disappearing ridership base caused by uninhibited interloping, and even curbside conflict among rival operators trying to pick up passengers. Better transit is readily available; we need only to organize policymakers to attain it.[2]

Our system would also give life to transit entrepreneurship. Within the property rights framework based on curb rights, entrepreneurs would be free, able, and perhaps even driven to introduce ever better service, revise schedules and route structures, establish connections among transit providers, facilitate passenger interchange between routes, introduce new vehicles, and use new pricing strategies. Alongside scheduled service, jitneys would respond flexibly to weather, time of day, special events, and other changing conditions. They would offer service on a short-term basis, fill market niches, provide courtesy door-to-door service, and simply pick up paying customers on the way to work. Once the system of curb rights was sensibly implemented, the market process would take over. One feature of this process is competition, but the other is discovery of new opportunities for service based on entrepreneurial insight into changing local conditions. Thus within a suitable framework of property rights the invisible hand will be able to do in transit what it does so well in other parts of the economy.

2. Further research is needed to understand the relationships between transit market conditions and suitable curb rights systems. For example, empirical research is needed to determine what sets of conditions are needed to make a market potentially thick. Viton (1988) and Viton and others (1982) study the conditions that make private *scheduled* service sustainable. It would be very useful to have studies of the conditions that make the jitney cascade self-sustaining.

References

Adler, Sy. 1991. "The Transformation of the Pacific Electric Railway: Bradford Snell, Roger Rabbit, and the Politics of Transportation in Los Angeles." *Urban Affairs Quarterly* 27 (1): 51–86.

Alchian, Armen A. 1950. "Uncertainty, Evolution and Economic Theory." *Journal of Political Economy* 58 (June): 211–21.

Altshuler, Alan. 1979. *The Urban Transportation System: Politics and Policy Innovation.* MIT Press.

American Public Transit Association. 1993. *Fact Book 1993.* Washington: American Public Transit Association.

Armstrong, Mark, Simeon Cowan, and John Vickers. 1994. *Regulatory Reform: Economic Analysis and British Experience.* MIT Press.

Bailey, Elizabeth E. 1981. "Contestability and the Design of Regulatory and Antitrust Policy." *American Economic Review* 71 (May): 178–83.

Bailey, Elizabeth E., and Ann F. Friedlaender. 1982. "Market Structure and Multiproduct Industries." *Journal of Economic Literature* 20 (September): 1024–48.

Banister, David. 1985. "Deregulating the Bus Industry in Britain: (A) The Proposals." *Transport Reviews* 5 (April–June): 99–103.

Banister, David and Laurie Pickup. 1990. "Bus Transport in the Metropolitan Areas and London." In Philip Bell and Paul Cloke, eds., *Deregulation and Transport: Market Forces in the Modern World*, 67–83. London: David Fulton Publishers.

Baumol, William J. 1967. "Macroeconomics of Unbalanced Growth: The Anatomy of Urban Crisis." *American Economic Review* 57 (June): 415–26.

Baumol, William J., John C. Panzar, and Robert Willig. 1982. *Contestable Markets and the Theory of Industry Structure.* Harcourt, Brace, Jovanovich.

Becker, A. Jeff, and James C. Echols. 1983. "Paratransit at a Transit Agency: The Experience in Norfolk, Virginia." *Transportation Research Record* 914: 49–57.

Beesley, M. E., and S. Glaister. 1985a. "Deregulating the Bus Industry in Britain: (C) A Response." *Transport Reviews* 5 (April–June): 133–42.

_____. 1985b. "Deregulating the Bus Industry in Britain: A Reply." *Transport Reviews* 5 (July–September): 223–24.

Beesley, Michael E., and Michael A. Kemp. 1987. "Urban Transportation." In Edwin S. Mills, ed., *Handbook of Regional and Urban Economics*, vol. 2: *Urban Economics*, 1023–52. North-Holland.

Beshers, Eric W. 1994. "External Costs of Automobile Travel and Appropriate Policy Responses." Highway Users Federation (March).

Blackburn, Robert, and Daniel Gilbert. 1995. *Photographic Enforcement of Traffic Laws*. TE 7. N36 219. Transportation Research Board.

Bly, P. H., and R. H. Oldfield. 1986. "Competition between Minibuses and Regular Bus Services." *Journal of Transportation Economics and Policy*, 20 (January): 47–68.

Boarnet, Marlon G. 1994. "Highways and Intrametropolitan Employment Location." University of California, Irvine, Department of Urban and Regional Planning.

Bonapace, Ruth. 1993. "Commuter War: Vans Battle Buses for Riders." *New York Times*, February 14: sec. 13, 1.

Boyle, David. 1993. "Jitney Enforcement Strategies in New York City." Paper prepared for the Seventy-Third Annual Meeting of Transportation Research Board.

Brown, Gerald R. 1972. "Analysis of User Preferences for System Characteristics to Cause a Modal Shift." *Highway Research Record* 417: 25–36.

Brownstone, David, and Thomas F. Golob. 1992. "The Effectiveness of Ridesharing Incentives: Discrete-Choice Models of Commuting in Southern California." *Regional Science and Urban Economics* 22 (March): 5–24.

Buchanan, James M., and Gordon Tullock. 1962. *The Calculus of Consent: Logical Foundations of Constitutional Democracy*. University of Michigan Press.

Caves, Douglas W., and others. 1985. "Network Effects and the Measurement of Returns to Scale and Density for U.S. Railroads." In Andrew F. Daughety, ed., *Analytical Studies in Transport Economics*, 97–120. Cambridge University Press.

Cervero, Robert. 1983. "Perceptions of Who Benefits from Public Transportation." *Transportation Research Record* 936: 15–19.

____. 1986. *Suburban Gridlock*. Berkeley, Calif.: Center for Urban Policy Research.

____. 1988. *Transit Service Contracting: Cream Skimming or Deficit Skimming*. Department of Transportation, Urban Mass Transit Administration.

____. 1996. "Jitneys, Vans, and Minibuses: Paratransit in America." University of California, Berkeley.

Chandler, Alfred D., with the assistance of H. Takashi. 1990. *Scale and Scope: The Dynamics of Industrial Capitalism*. Harvard University Press.

Chisholm, Donald. 1989. *Coordination without Hierarchy: Informal Structures in Multiorganizational Systems*. University of California Press.

Chomitz, Kenneth M., and Charles A. Lave. 1984. "Part-Time Labor, Work Rules, and Urban Transit Costs." *Journal of Transport Economics and Policy* 18 (January): 63–73.

Chou, Yue-Hong. 1992. "A Cluster Analysis of Disaggregate Decision-Making Processes in Travel Mode-Choice Behavior." *Transportation Planning and Technology* 16: 155–66.

Coase, Ronald H. 1937. "The Nature of the Firm." *Economica* 4 (November): 386–405.

Cohen, Linda R., and Roger G. Noll. 1994. "Privatizing Public Research." *Scientific American* 271 (September): 72–77.

Congressional Budget Office. 1988. *New Directions for the Nation's Public Works*.

Cooter, Robert D. 1996. "The Rule of State Law Versus the Rule-of-Law State: Economic Analysis of the Legal Foundations of Development." Paper presented at the Annual World Bank Conference on Develpment Economics.

Davis, Otto A., and Norman J. Johnson. 1984. "The Jitneys: A Study of Grassroots Capitalism." *Journal of Contemporary Studies* 7 (Winter): 81–102.

Demsetz, Harold. 1967. "Towards a Theory of Property Rights." *American Economic Association Papers and Proceedings* 57: 347–59.

____. 1968. "Why Regulate Utilities?" *Journal of Law and Economics* 11: 55–65.

De Soto, Hernando. 1989. *The Other Path: The Invisible Revolution in the Third World*, translated by June Abbott. Harper and Row.

Department of Transportation, Urban Mass Transportation Administration. 1984. "Private Enterprise Participation Program." *Federal Register* 49.

Department of Transportation. 1995. *National Transportation Statistics*. Bureau of Transportation Statistics.

Diandas, John, and Gabriel Roth. 1995. "Alternative Approaches to Improving Route Bus Services in Sri Lanka." Paper prepared for the Fourth International Conference on Competition and Ownership in Land Passenger Transport, Rotorua, New Zealand.

Dobson, Ricardo, and Gregory C. Nicolaidis. 1974. "Preferences for Transit Service by Homogeneous Groups of Individuals." General Motors Research Publication GMR-1616.

Dodgson, John S. 1991. "The Bus Industry and the Cases of Australia, the USA, and the U.K." In Kenneth Button and David Pitfield, eds., *Transport Deregulation: An International Movement*, 119–40. St. Martin's.

Dodgson, John S., and Y. Katsoulacos. 1991. "Competition, Contestability and Predation: The Economics of Competition in Deregulated Bus Markets." *Transportation Planning and Technology* 15: 263–75.

Downs, Anthony. 1992. *Stuck in Traffic: Coping with Peak-Hour Traffic Congestion*. Brookings.

Doxsey, Lawrence. 1986. "Interpreting the Results of Regulatory Revisions in Seattle and San Diego." *Transportation Research Record* 1103: 6–8.

Duffy, John Q. 1993. "Studies Indicate Deregulation Is a Bust." *Taxi* 38 (January-February): 22–23.

Eckert, Ross D. 1970. "The Los Angeles Taxi Monopoly: An Economic Inquiry." *Southern California Law Review* 43: 407–53.

____. 1973. "On the Incentives of Regulators: The Case of Taxicabs." *Public Choice* 14 (Spring): 83–99.

____. 1979. *California Transportation Planning: Examining the Entrails*. Los Angeles: International Institute for Economic Research.

Eckert, Ross D., and George W. Hilton. 1972. "The Jitneys." *Journal of Law and Economics* 15 (October): 293–325.

Federal Transit Authority. 1994. "Section 15 Data." Department of Transportation.

Feldstein, Dan. 1995. "Westheimers's Jitney Service Attempt Stalls." *Houston Chronicle*, July 11.

Ferguson, Tim W. 1995. "Who Said Anything about Transportation?" *Forbes* (December 4): 130f.

Fielding, Gordon. 1995. "Transit in American Cities." In Susan Hanson, ed., *Geography of Urban Transport*, 2d ed., 287–304. Guildford Press.

Fielding, Gordon J., and Daniel B. Klein. 1993. "How to Franchise Highways." *Journal of Transport Economics and Policy* 27 (May): 113–30.

Flannelly, Kevin J., and others. 1991. "Direct Comparison of Commuters' Interests in Using Different Modes of Transportation." *Transportation Research Record* 1321: 90–96.

Flink, James J. 1988. *The Automobile Age*. MIT Press.

Foster, Christopher, D. 1985. "The Economics of Bus Deregulation in Britain." *Transport Reviews* 5 (July-September): 207–14.

Frankena, Mark W., and Paul A. Pautler. 1986a. "Economic Analysis of Taxicab Regulation." *Transportation Research Record* 1103: 2–5.

——. 1986b. "Taxicab Regulation: An Economic Analysis." *Research in Law and Economics* 9: 129–65.

Fried, Joseph P. 1994. "A New Law Escalates the War against Unlicensed Vans." *New York Times*, February 13: A43.

Gardner, Marilyn. 1994. "After-School Vans Give Kids a Lift." *Christian Science Monitor*, January 13: 15.

Garreau, Joel. 1991. *Edge City: Life on the New Frontier*. Doubleday.

Garvin, Glenn. 1992. "Van Ban." *Reason* 24 (December): 53–55.

Giuliano, Genevieve. 1989. "New Directions for Understanding Transportation and Land Use." *Environment and Planning A* 21 (February): 145–59.

——. 1992. "Transportation Demand Management: Promise or Panacea?" *Journal of the American Planning Association* 58 (Summer): 327–35.

Giuliano, Genevieve, and Roger F. Teal. 1985. "Privately Provided Commuter Bus Services: Experiences, Problems, and Prospects." In Charles Lave, ed., *Urban Transit: The Private Challenge to Public Transportation*, 151–79. San Francisco: Pacific Institute for Public Policy Research.

——. 1987. "Estimating the Potential Cost Savings of Transit Service Contracting." *Transportation Research Record* 1108: 1–11.

Giuliano, Genevieve, Keith Hwang, and Martin Wachs. 1993. "Employee Trip Reduction in Southern California: First Year Results." *Transportation Research A* 27 (March): 125–37.

Goldberg, Victor P. 1976. "Regulation and Administered Contracts." *Bell Journal of Economics* 7 (Autumn): 426–48.

Golob, Thomas, and others. 1972. "An Analysis of Consumer Preferences for a Public Transportation System." *Transportation Research A* 6 (March): 81–102.

Gómez-Ibáñez, José A., and John R. Meyer. 1990. "Privatizing and Deregulating Local Public Services: Lessons from Britain's Buses." *Journal of the American Planning Association* 56 (Winter): 9–21.

——. 1993. *Going Private: The International Experience with Transport Privatization*. Brookings.

Gómez-Ibáñez, José A., and Kenneth A. Small. 1994. *Road Pricing for Congestion Management: A Survey of International Practice*. Washington: National Academy Press.

Gordon, Peter, and Harry Richardson. 1989. "Notes from Underground: The Failure of Urban Mass Transit." *Public Interest* 94 (Winter): 77–86.

Gordon, Peter, Harry W. Richardson, and Myung-Jin Jun. 1991. "The Commuting Paradox: Evidence from the Top Twenty." *Journal of the American Planning Association* 57 (Autumn): 416–20.

Graham, Cosmo, and Tony Prosser. 1991. *Privatizing Public Enterprises: Constitutions, the State, and Regulation in Comparative Perspective*. Clarendon Press.

Gramlich, Edward M. 1994. "Infrastructure Investment: A Review Essay." *Journal of Economic Literature* 32 (September): 1176–96.

Grava, Sigurd. 1980. "Paratransit in Developing Countries." In *Transportation and Development around the Pacific*, 278–89. New York: American Society of Civil Engineers.

Green, Kenneth. 1995. "Looking Beyond ECO: Alternatives to Employer-Based Trip Reduction." Policy Study 185. Los Angeles: Reason Foundation.

Gross, Jane. 1995. "Getting There the Hard Way, Every Day." *Los Angeles Times*, July 16: A1.

Gurza, Agustin. 1995. "'Tijuana Taxis' Are a Source of Livelihoods—and Friction." *Orange County Register*, February 20: 1.

Gwilliam, K. M., C. A. Nash, and P. J. Mackie. 1985a. "Deregulating the Bus Industry in Britain: (B) The Case Against." *Transport Reviews* 5 (April-June): 105–32.

——. 1985b. "Deregulating the Bus Industry in Britain: A Rejoinder." *Transport Reviews* 5 (July-September): 215–22.

Hamer, Andrew M., and Johannes F. Linn. 1987. "Urbanization in the Developing World: Patterns, Issues, and Policies." In Edwin S. Mills, ed., *Handbook of Regional and Urban Economics*, vol. 2: *Urban Economics*, 1255–84. North Holland Press.

Hahn, Robert W. 1984. "Market Power and Transferable Property Rights." *Quarterly Journal of Economics*, 99 (November): 753–65.

Hardin, Garrett. 1968. "The Tragedy of the Commons." *Science* 162 (December 13): 1243–48.

Hay, Alan. 1993. "Equity and Welfare in the Geography of Public Transport Provision." *Journal of Transport Geography* 6: 95–101.

Hayek, Friedrich A. 1944. *The Road to Serfdom*. University of Chicago Press.

——. 1960. *The Constitution of Liberty*. University of Chicago Press.

——. 1978. *New Studies in Philosophy, Politics, Economics and the History of Ideas*. University of Chicago Press.

Hazlett, Thomas. 1985. "The Curious Evolution of Natural Monopoly Theory." In Robert W. Poole, ed., *Unnatural Monopolies: The Case for Deregulating Public Utilities*, 1–25. Lexington, Mass.: Lexington Books.

Hensher, David A. 1988. "Productivity in Privately Owned and Operated Bus Firms in Australia." In J. S. Dodgson and N. Topham, eds., *Bus Deregulation and Privatization: An International Perspective*, 141–70. Aldershot, U.K.: Avebury.

Hensher, David. A., P. B. McLeod, and J. K. Stanley. 1975. "Usefulness of Attitudinal Measures in Investigating the Choice of Travel Mode." *International Journal of Transportation Economics* 2: 51–75.

Heramb, Cheri, Ashish Sen, and Siim Sööt. 1979. "Jitney Paratransit Services: An Appraisal of Present and Future Operations." *Transportation Research Record* 724: 1–8.

Hibbs, John. 1991. *The Liberalisation of the British Bus and Coach Industry: An Uncompleted Enterprise*. Economic Notes 38. London: Libertarian Alliance.

——. 1993. *On the Move . . . A Market for Mobility on the Roads*. London: Institute of Economic Affairs.

Hilton, George W. 1974. *Federal Transit Subsidies: The Urban Mass Transportation Assistance Program*. Washington: American Enterprise Institute.

——. "The Rise and Fall of Monopolized Transit." 1985. In Charles Lave, ed., *Urban Transit: The Private Challenge to Public Transportation*, 31–48. San Francisco: Pacific Institute for Public Policy Research.

Hodge, David C. 1988. "Fiscal Equity in Urban Mass Transit Systems: A Geographic Analysis." *Annals*, Association of American Geographers 78: 288–306.

Holtz-Eakin, Douglas. 1994. "Public Sector Capital and the Productivity Puzzle." *Review of Economics and Statistics* 76 (February): 12–21.

Johnson, Michael A. 1978. "Attribute Importance in Multiattribute Transportation Decisions." *Transportation Research Record* 673: 15–21.

Jones, David W. 1985. *Urban Transit Policy: An Economic and Political History*. Prentice-Hall.

Kain, John F. 1988. "Choosing the Wrong Technology: Or How to Spend Billions and Reduce Transit Use." *Journal of Advanced Transportation* 21 (Winter): 197–213.

____. 1990. "Deception in Dallas: Strategic Misrepresentation in Rail Transit Promotion and Evaluation." *Journal of the American Planning Association* 56 (Spring): 184–96.

Keeler, Theodore E. 1983. *Railroads, Freight, and Public Policy*. Brookings.

Kelejian, Harry H., and Dennis P. Robinson. 1994. "Infrastructure Productivity: A Razor's Edge." Working Paper. University of Maryland.

Kerin, Paul D. 1992. "Efficient Bus Fares." *Transport Reviews* 12 (January-March): 33–47.

Kirby, Ronald F. 1982. "Targeting Money Effectively: User-Side Transportation Subsidies." *Journal of Contemporary Studies* 4 (Spring): 45–52.

Kirby, Ronald, and others. 1974. *Para-Transit: Neglected Options for Urban Mobility*. Washington: Urban Institute.

Kirzner, Israel M. 1985. *Discovery and the Capitalist Process*. University of Chicago Press.

Klein, Benjamin, Robert G. Crawford, and Armen A. Alchian. 1978. "Vertical Integration, Appropriable Rents, and the Competitive Contracting Process." *Journal of Law and Economics* 21 (October): 297–326.

Klein, Daniel B. 1994. "If Government Is So Villainous, How Come Government Officials Don't Seem Like Villains?" *Economics and Philosophy* 10 (April): 91–106.

____. Forthcoming. "Trust for Hire: Voluntary Remedies for Quality and Safety." In Daniel B. Klein, ed., *Reputation: Studies in the Voluntary Elicitation of Good Conduct*. University of Michigan Press.

Klein, Daniel B., and Pia Maria Koskenoja. 1996. "The Smog-Reduction Road: Remote Sensing vs. the Clean Air Act." Policy Analysis 249. Washington: Cato Institute.

Kuzmyak, J. Richard, and Eric N. Schreffler. 1993. "Evaluation of the Effectiveness of Travel Demand Management Programs." In *Technical Papers from the Institute of Transportation Engineers' 1988, 1989, and 1990 Conferences*, 211–25. Institute of Transportation Engineers.

La Croix, Sumner J., James Mak, and Walter Miklius. 1985. "Evaluation of Alternative Arrangements for the Provision of Airport Taxi Service." *Logistics and Transportation Review* 28 (June): 147–66.

Lacey, Marc. 1994. "City Maps Better Cab Service for Neglected Areas." *Los Angeles Times*, September 3: B1.

LaGasse, Alfred B. III. 1986. "An Industry Comment on Regulatory Change." *Transportation Research Record* 1103: 19–23.

Lave, Charles A. 1977. "Rail Rapid Transit and Energy: The Adverse Effects." *Transportation Research Record* 648: 14–30.

Lave, Charles A., ed. 1985. *Urban Transit: The Private Challenge to Public Transportation*. San Francisco: Pacific Institute for Public Policy Research.

Lavoie, Don. 1985. *National Economic Planning: What Is Left?* Ballinger.

Lawson, Douglas R. 1993. "Passing the Test: Human Behavior and California's Smog Check Program." *Journal of the Air & Waste Management Association* 43 (December): 1567–75.

———. 1995. "The Costs of M in I/M: Reflections on Inspection/Maintenance Programs." *Journal of the Air & Waste Management Association* 45 (June): 465–76.

Levine, Ned, and Martin Wachs. 1986. "Bus Crime in Los Angeles, II: Victims and Public Impact." *Transportation Research A* 20 (July): 285–93.

Love, Jean, and Wendell Cox. 1991. "False Dreams and Broken Promises: The Wasteful Federal Investment in Urban Mass Transit." Policy Analysis 162. Washington: Cato Institute.

Lowe, Marcia D. 1990. "Alternatives to the Automobile: Transport for Livable Cities." Worldwatch Paper 98. Worldwatch Institute.

Machalaba, Daniel. 1991. "Opportunistic Vans Are Running Circles around City Buses." *Wall Street Journal*, July 24: A1.

Mackie, Peter, John Preston, and Chris Nash. 1995. "Bus Deregulation: Ten Years On." *Transport Reviews* 15 (July-August): 229–51.

Meyer, John R., and José Gómez-Ibáñez. 1981. *Autos, Transit, and Cities*. Harvard University Press.

Mises, Ludwig von. 1978. *Liberalism: A Socio-Economic Exposition*, translated by Ralph Raico. Kansas City: Sheed, Andrews, and McMeel.

Mitchell, Alison. 1992. "Vans Fighting a Strong Guerrilla War for New York's Streets." *New York Times*, January 24: A16.

Mohring, Herbert. 1972. "Optimization and Scale Economies in Urban Bus Transportation." *American Economic Review* 62 (September): 591–604.

Morlok, Edward K., and Philip A.Viton. 1985. "The Comparative Costs of Public and Private Providers of Mass Transit." In Charles Lave, ed., *Urban Transit: The Private Challenge to Public Transportation*, 233–53. San Francisco: Pacific Institute for Public Policy Research.

Morris, D. J., and others. 1986. "Strategic Behaviour and Industrial Competition: An Introduction." *Oxford Economic Papers* 38 supp. (November): 1–8.

Mueller, Dennis C. 1989. *Public Choice II*. Cambridge University Press.

Nash, Christopher A. 1988. "Integration of Public Transport: An Economic Assessment." In J. S. Dodgson and N. Topham, eds., *Bus Deregulation and Privatisation: An International Perspective*, 97–233. Aldershot, U.K.: Avebury.

Nationwide Personal Transportation Survey. 1990. *1990 NPTS Databook*. Federal Highway Administration, Office of Highway Information Management.

Niskanen, William A. 1971. *Bureaucracy and Representative Government*. Chicago: Aldine-Atherton.

Office of Highway Information Management. 1993. *Transportation Energy Data Book: Edition 15*. Oakridge, Tenn.: Department of Transportation.

Office of Management and Budget. 1992. "Guidelines and Discount Rates for Benefit-Cost Analysis of Federal Programs." Circular A-94, revised (transmittal memo 64, October 29).

O'Leary, Katherine. 1982. "Planning for New and Integrated Demand-Responsive Systems." In Herbert S. Levinson and Robert A. Weant, *Urban Transportation: Perspectives and Prospects*, 317–21. Westport, Conn.: ENO Foundation.

Olsen, William T., and Seward Smith. 1973. *Psychological Implications of Public Transportation Service*. Florida State University, Department of Urban and Regional Planning.

Olsson, Marie L., and J. Richard Kuzmyak. 1985. *A Summary of the Operating Experience of the Indianapolis Jitney Express*. Federal Transit Administration, Technical Assistance Program.

Onishi, Norimitsu. 1994. "Bus Fare Dips $1 to Attract Livery Riders." *New York Times*, September 25: sec. 13, 10.

Orski, C. Kenneth. 1990. "Can Management of Travel Demand Help Solve Our Growing Traffic Congestion and Air Pollution Problems?" *Transportation Quarterly* 44 (October): 483–98.

Pashigian, Peter. 1976. "Consequences and Causes of Public Ownership of Urban Transit Facilities." *Journal of Political Economy* 84 (December): 1239–59.

Perry, James L., Timlynn Babitsky, and Hal Gregersen. 1988. "Organizational Form and Performance in Urban Mass Transit." *Transportation Reviews* 8 (April-June): 125–43.

Pickrell, Donald H. 1992. "A Desire Named Streetcar: Fantasy and Fact in Rail Transit Planning." *Journal of the American Planning Association* 58 (Spring): 158–76.

Poole, Robert W., Jr., and Philip E. Fixler Jr. 1987. "Privatization of Public-Sector Services in Practice: Experience and Potential." *Journal of Policy Analysis and Management* 6 (Summer): 612–25.

Poole, Robert W., Jr., and Michael Griffin. 1994. "Shuttle Vans: The Overlooked Transit Alternative." Policy Study 176. Los Angeles: Reason Foundation.

Primeaux, Walter J. 1976. "An Assessment of X-Efficiency Gained through Competition." *Review of Economics and Statistics*: 105–08.

Public Utilities Commission (PUC). 1918. *9th Annual Report*. Los Angeles.

Pucher, John. 1993a. "Social and Environmental Costs of Automobile Driving." *Passenger Transport* 51 (November 8): 1, 5.

_____. 1993b. "Strategies for Raising the Price of Auto Use to Reflect Its Full Cost." *Passenger Transport* 51 (November 15): 5.

Pucher, John, Anders Markstedt, and Ira Hirschman. 1983. "Impacts of Subsidies on the Costs of Urban Public Transport." *Journal of Transport Economics and Policy* (May): 155–76.

Rehmke, Greg. 1991. "McTransit for the 1990's." *Econ Update* (March): 3f.

Reinke, David. 1986. "Update on Taxicab and Jitney Regulation in San Diego." *Transportation Research Record* 1103: 9–11.

Richmond, Jonathan E. D. Forthcoming. *Transport of Delight: The Mythical Conception of Rail Transit in Los Angeles*. Johns Hopkins University Press.

Rimmer, Peter. 1988. "Buses in Southeast Asian Cities: Privatisation without Deregulation." In J. S. Dodgson and Neil Topham, eds., *Bus Deregulation and Privatisation: An International Perspective*, 185–208. Aldershot, U.K.: Avebury.

Rosenbloom, Sandi. 1972. "Taxis and Jitneys: The Case for Deregulation." *Reason* (February): 4–16.

Rosenbloom, Sandra. 1981. "Urban Taxi Policies." *Journal of Contemporary Studies* (Spring): 71–81.

_____. 1985. "The Taxi in the Urban Transport System." In Charles A. Lave, ed., *Urban Transit: The Private Challenge to Public Transportation*, 181–213. San Francisco: Pacific Institute for Public Policy Research.

_____. 1986. "Lessons for Policy Makers." *Transportation Research Record* 1103: 15–19.

Roth, Gabriel. 1987. *The Private Provision of Public Services in Developing Countries.* Oxford University Press.

Roth, Gabriel, and Anthony Shephard. 1984. *Wheels within Cities: New Alternatives for Passenger Transport.* London: Adam Smith Institute.

Rothschild, Michael, and Joseph E. Stiglitz. 1976. "Equilibrium in Competitive Insurance Markets: An Essay on the Economics of Imperfect Information." *Quarterly Journal of Economics* 90 (November): 630–49.

Rottenberg, Simon. 1985. "Job Protection in Urban Mass Transit." *Cato Journal* 5 (Spring-Summer): 239–58.

Sale, James E., and Bryan Green. 1979. "Operating Costs and Performance of American Public Transit Systems." *American Planning Association Journal* 45 (January): 22–27.

Saltzman, Arthur, and Richard J. Solomon. 1973. "Jitney Operations in the United States." *Highway Research Record* 449: 63–70.

Savage, Ian. 1985. *Deregulation of Bus Services.* Aldershot, U.K.: Gower.

——. 1986. "Evaluation of Competition in the British Local Bus Industry." *Transportation Research Record* 1064: 1–10.

——. 1993. "Deregulation and Privatization of Britain's Local Bus Industry." *Journal of Regulatory Economics:* 143–58.

Savas, E. S. 1982. *Privatizing the Public Sector: How to Shrink Government.* Chatham House.

Shipe, Richard Thomas. 1992. "Cost and Productivity in the U. S. Urban Bus Transit Sector, 1978-1989." Ph.D. dissertation, University of California, Berkeley.

Smith, Adam. 1937 (1776). *The Wealth of Nations.* Modern Library.

Smith, Rodney T., Arthur S. De Vany, and Robert J. Michaels. 1990. "Defining a Right of Access to Interstate Natural Gas Pipelines." *Contemporary Policy Issues* 8 (April): 142–58.

Starkie, David. 1993. "Train Service Co-ordination in a Competitive Market." *Fiscal Studies* 14 (2): 53–64.

Stevenson, Richard. 1993. "Will Minicab Force Mighty Taxi off the Road?" *New York Times,* July 16: A4.

Stigler, George J. 1971. "The Theory of Economic Regulation." *Bell Journal of Economics and Management Science* (Spring): 3–21.

Straszheim, Mahlon R. 1979. "Assessing the Social Costs of Urban Transportation Technologies." In Peter Mieszkowski and Mahlon Straszheim, eds., *Current Issues in Urban Economics,* 196–232. Johns Hopkins University Press.

Styring, Bill. 1994. "How Indianapolis Won the War of the Taxis." *Indiana Policy Review* (December): 31–35.

Suzuki, Peter. 1985. "Vernacular Cabs: Jitneys and Gypsies in Five Cities." *Transportation Research A* 19: 337–47.

——. 1995. "Unregulated Taxicabs." *Transportation Quarterly* 49 (Winter): 12–38.

Takyi, Isaac K. 1990. "An Evaluation of Jitney Systems in Developing Countries." *Transportation Quarterly* 44 (January): 163–77.

Talley, Wayne K. 1991. "Contracting Out and Cost Economies for a Public Transit Firm." *Transportation Quarterly* 45 (July): 409–20.

Taylor, Brian D. 1992. "When Finance Leads Planning: The Influence of Public Finance on Transportation Planning and Policy in California." Ph.D. dissertation, University of California, Los Angeles.

Teal, Roger F. 1986. "Impacts of Comprehensive Urban Transportation Deregulation in Arizona." *Transportation Research Record* 1103: 11–14.

_____. 1988. "Public Transit Service Contracting: A Status Report." *Transportation Quarterly* 42 (April): 207–22.

Teal, Roger F., and Mary Berglund. 1987. "The Impacts of Taxi Deregulation in the USA." *Journal of Transport Economics and Policy* 21 (January): 37–56.

Teal, Roger F., and Terry Nemer. 1986. "Privatization of Urban Transit: The Los Angeles Jitney Experience." *Transportation* 13: 5–22.

Teal, Roger F., James V. Marks, and Richard Goodhue. 1979. *Subsidized Shared-Ride Taxi Services.* Institute of Transportation Studies Working Paper 79-2. University of California, Irvine.

Teal, Roger, and others. 1984. *Private Sector Options for Commuter Transportation.* UMTA-CA-11-0022-1. Department of Transportation.

Tehan, Claire, and Martin Wachs. 1972. *The Role of Psychological Needs in Mass Transit.* Urban Planning Report. University of California, Los Angeles.

Tramontozzi, Paul N., and Kenneth W. Chilton. 1987. *The Federal Free Ride: The Economics and Politics of U.S. Transit Policy.* Washington University, Center for the Study of American Business.

Transportation Research Board. 1988. *New Organizational Responses to the Changing Transit Environment: Proceedings of a Conference in Norfolk, Va., December 2–4, 1987.* Washington.

Transportation Systems Center. 1982. "An Overview of Paratransit." In Herbert S. Levinson and Robert A. Weant, eds., *Urban Transportation Perspectives and Prospects,* 303–17. Westport, Conn.: ENO Foundation.

Tucker, Jeffrey R. 1993. "Notes from the Underground: America's Sprawling Informal Economy." *Policy Review* (Summer): 76–79.

Tullock, Gordon. 1967. "The Welfare Costs of Tariffs, Monopolies and Theft." *Western Economic Journal* 5: 224–32.

Turner, Daniel S. 1994. "Video Evidence for Highway Tort Trials." *Transportation Research Record* 1464: 86–91.

Urban Mobility Corporation. 1992. *The Miami Jitneys.* Federal Transit Administration, Office of Private Sector Initiatives.

Vickers, John, and George Yarrow. 1991. "Economic Perspectives on Privatization." *Journal of Economic Perspectives* 5 (Spring): 111–32.

Viton, Philip. A. 1981. "A Translog Cost Function for Urban Bus Transit." *Journal of Industrial Economics* 29 (March): 287–304.

_____. 1988. *Evaluating the Feasibility and Desirablility of Transit Deregulation,* vols. 1 and 2. Report OH-11-0007-88-1. Department of Transportation, Urban Mass Transit Administration.

Viton, Philip, and others. 1982. *The Feasibility and Desirablility of Privately Provided Transit Services.* Department of Transportation, Urban Mass Transit Administration.

Wachs, Martin. 1992. "Can Transit Be Saved? Of Course It Can!" Address prepared for the Metropolitan Conference on Public Transportation Research, Chicago.

Walder, Jay H. 1985. "Private Commuter Vans in New York." In Charles Lave, ed., *Urban Transit: The Private Challenge to Public Transportation,* 101–19. San Francisco: Pacific Institute for Public Policy Research.

Walters, Alan A. 1979. "Privatization in British Transport Policy." In John C. Weicker, ed., *Private Innovations in Public Transit*, 101–08. Washington: American Enterprise Institute.

Webber, Melvin M. 1976. "The BART Experience: What Have We Learned?" *Public Interest* 45 (Fall): 79–108.

———. 1992. "The Joys of Automobility." In Martin Wachs and Margaret Crawford, eds., *The Car and the City: The Automobile, the Environment, and Daily Urban Life*, 274–84. University of Michigan Press.

———. 1994. "The Marriage of Autos and Transit: How to Make Transit Popular Again." *Access* 5.

Weiner, Edward. 1982. "The Characteristics, Uses, and Potentials of Taxicab Transportation." In Herbert S. Levinson and Robert A. Weant, eds., *Urban Transportation: Perspectives and Prospects*, 322–29. Westport, Conn.: ENO Foundation.

Weingast, Barry R., Kenneth A. Shepsle, and Christopher Johnsen. 1981. "The Political Economy of Benefits and Costs: A Neoclassical Approach to Distributive Politics." *Journal of Political Economy* 89 (August): 642–64.

Weisman, Mark. 1981. "Variables Influencing Transit Use." *Traffic Quarterly* 35 (July): 371–83.

———. 1984. "Advertising Transit Shelter Program." *Transportation Quarterly* 38 (July): 361–74.

White, Peter R. 1992. "Three Years' Experience of Bus Service Deregulation in Britain." In Antti Talvitie, David Hensher, and Michael Beesley, eds., *Privatization and Deregulation in Passenger Transportation*, 43–60. Helsinki: University of Tampere.

———. 1995. "Deregulation of Local Bus Services in Great Britain: An Introductory Review." *Transport Reviews* 15 (April–June): 185–209.

Williamson, Oliver E. 1979. "Transaction-Cost Economics: The Governance of Contractual Relations." *Journal of Law and Economics* 22 (October): 233–61.

———. 1985. *The Economic Institutions of Capitalism: Firms, Markets, and Relational Contracting*. Free Press.

Wohl, Martin. 1982. "Increasing the Taxi's Role in Urban America." In Herbert S. Levinson and Robert A. Weant, eds., *Urban Transportation: Perspectives and Prospects*, 329–32. Westport, Conn.: ENO Foundation.

World Bank. 1988. *Urban Transit*. World Bank Policy Study.

Young, Karen Newell. 1995. "Shuttle Endeavor." *Los Angeles Times*, September 22: E1, E6.

Zimmerman, Robert. 1992. "New York's War against the Vans." *Freeman* (April): 150–51.

Index

CPSIA information can be obtained at www.ICGtesting.com
Printed in the USA
LVOW061022210112

264964LV00002B/253/P